The American Revolution

Other Books in the Turning Points Series:

Turning|Points

IN WORLD HISTORY

The American Revolution

Kirk D. Werner, *Book Editor*

David L. Bender, *Publisher*
Bruno Leone, *Executive Editor*
Bonnie Szumski, *Editorial Director*
David M. Haugen, *Managing Editor*

Greenhaven Press, Inc., San Diego, California

Every effort has been made to trace the owners of copyrighted material. The articles in this volume may have been edited for content, length, and/or reading level. The titles have been changed to enhance the editorial purpose.

Library of Congress Cataloging-in-Publication Data

The American Revolution / Kirk D. Werner, book editor.
    p.   cm. — (Turning points in world history)
  Includes bibliographical references (p.   ) and index.
  ISBN 0-7377-0238-9 (pbk. : alk. paper). —
ISBN 0-7377-0239-7 (lib. : alk. paper)
  1. United States—History—Revolution, 1775–1783. I. Werner, Kirk D. II. Series: Turning points in world history (Greenhaven Press)
E208.A43 2000
973.3—dc21   99-38377
                                                                  CIP

Cover photo: Peter Newark's American Pictures

©2000 by Greenhaven Press, Inc.
P.O. Box 289009, San Diego, CA 92198-9009

Printed in the U.S.A.

Contents

some revolutionaries could be considered reluctant participants in the battles to come.

people behind a cause. The stories that circulated about the war enraged and incited both the British and the Americans.

Foreword

Certain past events stand out as pivotal, as having effects and outcomes that change the course of history. These events are often referred to as turning points. Historian Louis L. Snyder provides this useful definition:

> A turning point in history is an event, happening, or stage which thrusts the course of historical development into a different direction. By definition a turning point is a great event, but it is even more—a great event with the explosive impact of altering the trend of man's life on the planet.

History's turning points have taken many forms. Some were single, brief, and shattering events with immediate and obvious impact. The invasion of Britain by William the Conqueror in 1066, for example, swiftly transformed that land's political and social institutions and paved the way for the rise of the modern English nation. By contrast, other single events were deemed of minor significance when they occurred, only later recognized as turning points. The assassination of a little-known European nobleman, Archduke Franz Ferdinand, on June 28, 1914, in the Bosnian town of Sarajevo was such an event; only after it touched off a chain reaction of political-military crises that escalated into the global conflict known as World War I did the murder's true significance become evident.

Other crucial turning points occurred not in terms of a few hours, days, months, or even years, but instead as evolutionary developments spanning decades or even centuries. One of the most pivotal turning points in human history, for instance—the development of agriculture, which replaced nomadic hunter-gatherer societies with more permanent settlements—occurred over the course of many generations. Still other great turning points were neither events nor developments, but rather revolutionary new inventions and innovations that significantly altered social customs and ideas, military tactics, home life, the spread of knowledge, and the human condition in general. The developments of writing, gunpowder, the printing press, antibiotics, the electric light, atomic energy, television, and the computer, the last two of which have recently ushered in the world-altering information age, represent only some of these innovative turning points.

Each anthology in the Greenhaven Turning Points in World History series presents a group of essays chosen for their accessibility. The anthology's structure also enhances this accessibility. First, an introductory essay provides a general overview of the principal events and figures involved, placing the topic in its historical context. The essays that follow explore various aspects in more detail, some targeting political trends and consequences, others social, literary, cultural, and/or technological ramifications, and still others pivotal leaders and other influential figures. To aid the reader in choosing the material of immediate interest or need, each essay is introduced by a concise summary of the contributing writer's main themes and insights.

In addition, each volume contains extensive research tools, including a collection of excerpts from primary source documents pertaining to the historical events and figures under discussion. In the anthology on the French Revolution, for example, readers can examine the works of Rousseau, Voltaire, and other writers and thinkers whose championing of human rights helped fuel the French people's growing desire for liberty; the French *Declaration of the Rights of Man and Citizen*, presented to King Louis XVI by the French National Assembly on October 2, 1789; and eyewitness accounts of the attack on the royal palace and the horrors of the Reign of Terror. To guide students interested in pursuing further research on the subject, each volume features an extensive bibliography, which for easy access has been divided into separate sections by topic. Finally, a comprehensive index allows readers to scan and locate content efficiently. Each of the anthologies in the Greenhaven Turning Points in World History series provides students with a complete, detailed, and enlightening examination of a crucial historical watershed.

Introduction: "These Are the Times That Try Men's Souls"

The effects of the American Revolution reached far beyond the British colonies in North America. The ideals that drove the revolution and inspired its leaders were embraced within decades in France and later in other, more remote parts of the world as the concepts of liberty and equality informed the political consciousness of the world. But though revolutions may be made by philosophers or politicians, rarely are they won by them. The majority of the American colonists had no desire to overthrow the British government; and, in fact, many were quite content with their treatment under British rule for the first hundred-plus years of North American settlement. Taxes were low, many colonies had local legislative bodies with broad authority to handle day-to-day administration, and the British government was very helpful in protecting the colonies from both European and Native American threats. So what caused content British subjects to rise up in arms against their mother country and throw off the reins of the British Empire? The answer is not simple. But it is possible to trace building tensions long before a few fateful nights in 1776. Noted historian R.R. Palmer describes the American Revolution as

> a great event for the whole Eur-American world. In the Age of Democratic Revolution the American Revolution was . . . the earliest successful assertion of the principle that public power must arise from those over whom it is exercised. . . . Its effect on the area of Western Civilization came in part from the inspiration of its message.[1]

The Start of an Imperial Crisis

Most historians start their discussion of the road to the American Revolution in the 1760s. The British and the French were engaged in the Seven Years' War, a war which spilled into the colonies of North America and was known there as the French and Indian War. After the defeat of the French and their allies, the British Empire in North America was much larger than before, now comprising all territory between the Atlantic Ocean and the Mississippi. But Britain was not prepared to manage these vast lands or the inhabitants therein. In an effort to slow the spread of British settlement into these uncontrolled and recently contested lands, the king signed the Royal Proclamation of 1763. This legislation drew a line along the Appalachian Mountains, beyond which colonists were forbidden. Colonial governments were likewise forbidden to send survey teams to scout the area. Official and unofficial resentment of the restriction began to grow, and a larger issue would soon intensify that resentment.

The British government had incurred considerable debt fighting the Seven Years' War in both Europe and North America. For the twenty-five-year-old British monarch, George III, lowering the national debt was the most important item on the political agenda. During the war, the British debt had almost doubled, from £75 million to £137 million; interest alone on this debt was more than £5 million. While many parts of the British Empire were rather heavily taxed, the colonies of North America had been largely spared this burden. The king's chief minister, George Grenville, evaluated possible sources of revenue and concluded that the colonies should bear a larger share of the cost of their defense. In 1763 the colonists paid about £1,600 in trade duties, while the British government spent more than £8,000 to operate the customs service alone.

In 1764, Grenville used his considerable influence in the British Parliament to pass several acts to control the colonies. The first, the Sugar Act, consisted of several regulations governing the loading and unloading of trading vessels. It also placed significant trade duties on colonial imports such as coffee, indigo, sugar, and wine. Grenville expected an increase of £40,000 in yearly revenue from the Sugar Act. The second parliamentary act was the Currency Act, which concerned the printing of paper money in the colonies. The colonies were constantly short of money. To make up the shortage, colonial legislatures issued their own paper money, which British leaders feared would adversely affect the value of British currency. The Currency Act of 1764 prohibited the printing of paper money in all the colonies.[2] The result was a decline in the value of circulating colonial currency, since no one was obligated to accept it in payment of debts. This deflation, along with the new duties of the Sugar Act, had a devastating effect on the economy of the North American colonies.

The colonial response to the new British policies was swift. One of the most significant responses was the publication of a pamphlet by James Otis Jr. titled *The Rights of British Colonies, Asserted and Proved*. The pamphlet begins:

> The origin of government has in all ages no less perplexed the heads of lawyers and politicians, than the origin of evil has embarrassed divines and philosophers: and 'tis probable the world may receive a satisfactory solution on both those points of enquiry at the same time.[3]

Otis wrote the tract to educate readers in New England of their rights as Englishmen. He also wished to show the British government that the colonists of North America, not mindless followers of British policy, deserved a voice in the political arena. His message did not go unheeded, as political opposition to Grenville in Parliament found common ground with the colonies, and a cry went up for proper representation for all British colonial citizens.

The Stamp Act

Grenville was unmoved by this argument and continued to push legislation to increase tax revenues from the colonies. His next step would draw unified opposition from the colonies; for the first time, Parliament asserted its full power to impose direct taxes on the colonies. The Stamp Act, as the tax was called, required the colonists to buy and affix stamps for almost every printed page, from newspapers and almanacs to wills and playing cards. The amount of tax varied with the value of the material and had to be paid in hard currency (not the aforementioned paper money of the colonies). Grenville justified the new tax act on three grounds: First, the citizens of England had been paying a stamp tax on their printed materials for years; second, each subject in Britain paid more than twenty times the amount that colonists paid in taxes; and third, Grenville believed that the concept of "virtual representation" answered the argument of "taxation without representation" from the colonists. He maintained that all members of Parliament spoke for all parts of the empire, not just for a single district.

Many leaders in Parliament supported Grenville's idea to tax the colonies in North America but understood that a direct tax such as this would anger the colonists. Grenville asked colonial leaders, including Benjamin Franklin, to predict colonial reaction. Though Franklin's own livelihood as the premier newspaper printer in the colonies was affected by the Stamp Act, he told Grenville that colonial reaction would not be so violet as to cause undue trouble. Franklin was sadly mistaken.

Reaction to the news of the Stamp Act was slow in building but its direct influence on the growing newspaper industry caused printers to organize their own resistance. Letters and articles about the Stamp Act were passed from region to region and soon groups of colonists were formed to stand against the British Parliament's actions. One of the first of these groups was the Loyal Nine, which would later manifest itself as the Sons of Liberty, led by Samuel Adams. Protests ranged from simple letter writing campaigns to tarring and feathering stamp tax collectors. The Virginia House of Burgesses heard a young lawyer, Patrick Henry, speak out against the British Parliament in very direct terms, denying its authority to impose taxes on the colonies at all. Many newspapers reprinted Henry's resolutions, and his words spread throughout North America. Other colonial leaders organized the Stamp Act Congress in October 1765 to call for intercolonial resistance to the taxation.

British authorities had very little choice but to repeal the Stamp Act in 1766, but by then the damage had been done. Colonists throughout North America were aware of the ill will between the British and the colonial legislatures. Parliament passed the Declaratory Act in 1766, which asserted that colonial legislatures did not have the "sole and exclusive right of imposing taxes and duties," and that Parliament was the final authority in legislative matters in the colony. The standoff between political leaders on both shores had begun.

The Clouds Begin to Build

When King George III called for a new cabinet in 1766, hopes rose in the colonies for a cooling of hostilities between Mother England and North America. It was not to be. The newly appointed chancellor of the exchequer was Charles Townshend, confident in his ability to tax the colonies effectively. Townshend advocated indirect taxation of the North American colonies via import duties on British-manufactured products such as glass, paper, lead, and tea. To circumvent these new duties, American merchants turned to smuggling these products into colonial ports in Dutch ships.

Resistance among the general population increased as well. Samuel Adams and other colonial leaders advocated a policy called "nonimportation," in which the taxed products were replaced with products produced in the colonies. Historian Pauline Maier describes this policy as

> offering the "wisest and only peaceable method" for Americans to recover their liberty, one, moreover, that was legal and seemed to promise success. As during the Stamp Act crisis, colonists argued that economic retrenchment would awaken the attention of [the] British.[4]

But not all resistance was peaceful. In the spring of 1770, gangs of men and boys roamed the streets of Boston, coercing merchants by threat and force into supporting the boycott. The colonial governor called for British troops to control the streets, and confrontation was inevitable. On March 5, 1770, in front of the customs house, a rough mob began taunting the soldiers, pelting them with snowballs and rocks. Tension grew until one of the soldiers was knocked to the ground. As he struggled to rise, he fired a shot from his weapon and general firing broke out. When the smoke of musket fire cleared, five men lay dead and dying. The leaders of the colonial resistance hailed these fallen men as heroes, and called for the blood of the soldiers to redress what soon was called the Boston Massacre.

Sympathy for protestors grew and increased resistance led the British to rescind the Townshend duties except for the tax on tea. Colonists asked themselves how far their king and Parliament were willing to go to control them.

The Beginning of the End

By 1772 tensions in the colonies had subsided somewhat. Lord North had replaced Townshend and sought to avoid new confrontations with the American colonies by not proposing challenging legislation. The population of the colonies had grown to over 2 million inhabitants, with several colonial cities, including Philadelphia and Boston, ranked among the largest cities in the British Empire. Generations had established themselves on colonial soil by then, however, and colonists' identification with an American homeland was growing.

Local incidents began to raise tensions again in 1772. When a Royal Navy vessel, the *Gaspée*, ran aground chasing smugglers near Rhode Island, some colonists dressed up as Native Americans and burned the ship. British officials were outraged and offered a reward for identifying the culprits, but local officials did nothing, as it was understood that the perpetrators would be sent back to England for trial, rather than prosecuted locally. Samuel Adams dispersed rumor and information about this and other issues through underground committees of correspondence, groups that proliferated in the colonies at this time.

The final straw, as some colonists saw it, was the Tea Act of 1773. Lord North was trying to boost the revenues of the East India Company, the joint-stock company that controlled most British trading interests in India. The act stated that the British tea ships would trade directly with the colonies, bypassing colonial merchants and competing directly with Dutch tea. North seemed completely unaware of the impact in lost profits that this legislation would have on the British colonies of North America. Once more the port city of Boston would become the center of the storm of rebellion in North America.

When the first ship bringing British tea docked at Boston, Samuel Adams and other leaders in the committee of correspondence in Massachusetts were ready. For more than two weeks, the ship sat at anchor waiting for a British official to come and take possession of the cargo. Popular support had rallied behind the Adams faction and no one came forward. On December 16 local leaders determined to either force the ship from port or take drastic action against it. When the former tactic was unsuccessful, several dozen men dressed as Native Americans dumped 342 chests of tea, valued at over £10,000, into Boston harbor.

The Boston Tea Party shocked Lord North, unused to direct confrontation with the colonists, into passage of the Coercive Acts of 1774. The first act, the Boston Port Bill, closed the port of Boston, making all trade illegal until the bill for the tea had been paid. The next two acts suspended the royal charter of Massachusetts, expanded the power of the royal governor, abolished the elective council, and replaced this council with a body of men chosen by the Crown.

The final indignity was an expansion of the Quartering Act of 1765 that allowed the royal governor, General Thomas Gage, to house his troops in any unoccupied dwelling, even homes, as long as rent was paid. Gage proceeded to bring several hundred troops to Boston in line with these new laws.

The Coercive Acts (or Intolerable Acts, as the Boston press called them) were aimed at Boston only, but their impact was far-reaching. Historian Norman K. Risjord explains:

> The Coercive Acts . . . were directed primarily at Massachusetts; they were a violent, but probably temporary, effort to punish the vandalism of Boston. Yet they involved an implied threat to all the colonies. Closing the port of Boston and quartering troops on private households were actions without precedent in English or American experience. . . . Colonial Rights were being lost, not by a direct frontal assault, but by gradual attrition—like the slicing of a sausage—and the need for a united stand was evident.[5]

Between May 17 and May 23, colonial leaders in Providence, New York, and Philadelphia, along with those in Boston, called for an intercolonial congress to decide on a common course of action.

The First Continental Congress

In the first overt act of political rebellion, the committees of correspondence organized the First Continental Congress in Philadelphia on September 5, 1774. Every colony except Georgia sent representatives. Among the fifty-six delegates present were Samuel Adams and his younger cousin John, Patrick Henry, and George Washington. Their overt goal was to determine a unified response to the recent legislation against Boston. A smaller group within the congress, with Samuel Adams as its spokesman, wanted to prepare the colonies for all-out rebellion against the British. Their plan was presented in a document called the Suffolk Resolves, which was approved by the congress and represented the first step to a military showdown with British forces in North America. It also committed the members of the congress to uphold an economic boycott of British goods, as well as the continuation of nonexportation of colonial products if Parliament did not rescind the Coercive or Intolerable Acts.

Faced with this bold defiance, many people in the colonies felt forced to choose between remaining loyal to the British government that had controlled them for 150 years or moving closer to an independent colonial government. Those who supported the British thought of themselves as loyalists, though the other colonists called them Tories. At the congress, only a few voices of the loyalist cause were heard. One in particular, Joseph Galloway of Pennsylvania, proposed a solution that would keep the British in control but give a greater voice to the colonial representatives. The more radical majority contingent of the Continental Congress called his plan impractical and struck it from the record.

By the end of the year, colonial North America was preparing for a direct confrontation with the world's dominant power. While outwardly they seemed optimistic, even confident, inwardly many colonists still held out hope that this show of defiance would convince the British government to treat colonial interests and rights seriously. Unfortunately, the British government completely ignored the First Continental Congress and treated the colonists like spoiled children, perhaps underestimating the seriousness of their resolve.

"Give Me Liberty or Give Me Death"

The months between the Continental Congress and the fateful battles of the spring of 1775 found loyalists in North America terrified. Often pulled from their houses to be tarred and feathered, they pleaded with British officials to put down mobs of rebellious colonists. In February 1775 the British government declared that the colony of Massachusetts was in a state of rebellion, and as such had forfeited its rights under British law. But despite this declaration, British officials were still not convinced of the strength or unity of colonial activism. Historians George B. Tindall and David E. Shi describe this period as chaotic and dangerous:

> The militia, as much a social as a military organization in the past, now took to serious drill in formations, tactics, and marksmanship, and organized special units of Minute Men ready for quick mobilization. Everywhere royal officials were losing control as provincial congresses assumed authority and colonial militias organized and gathered arms and gunpowder. But British military officials remained smugly confident. Maj. John Pitcairn wrote home from Boston in March: "I am satisfied that one active campaign, a smart action, and burning two or three of their towns, will set everything to rights."[6]

British opinion drastically changed on March 23, 1775. From the floor of the Virginia legislature, Patrick Henry, already known as a revolutionary in the colonies, put a decisive stamp on the conflict. In a fiery speech, Henry put into words the impulse toward rebellion:

> Is life so dear, or peace so sweet, as to be purchased at the price of chains and slavery? Forbid it, Almighty God! I know not what course others may take; but as for me, give me liberty or give me death![7]

The Shot Heard 'Round the World

As rebellious sentiment swept through the colonies, British officials prepared to meet uprisings. In April, General Gage was instructed by the Crown to suppress rebellion (which was still seen as a Massachusetts issue) with all necessary force. Gage enlarged his forces in Boston and called for reinforcements. The local revolutionaries saw the troop buildup as direct aggression against the colonies and organized a warning system to track British military movements into Boston. From the Old North Church on April 18, 1775, the famous signal of lamps was clearly visible, and Paul Revere, along with William Davis, rode through the countryside toward Concord to warn the people of the battle to come. British troops had been ordered to march to Concord to seize the military arsenal there. In their path stood 70 Minutemen, who supposedly wished only to observe and slow the British. When the two groups faced off across the village green of Lexington, a mysterious shot, the "shot heard 'round the world," became the first shot of the American Revolution on April 19, 1775. In the first day of fighting, between Lexington and Concord, 95 colonists and more than 250 British soldiers died. The soldiers came under constant fire from local militia forces and unorganized farmers and would have been wiped out without reinforcements from Boston. With this clear indication of the seriousness of the colonial stance, Britain turned to putting down the rebellion.

As news of the bloodshed coursed through New England and beyond, colonial leadership divided quickly into moderates and radicals, with the moderates in the majority. The Second Continental Congress convened in Philadelphia in May 1775 as military clashes with the British were taking place, but many delegates hoped full-scale revolution could still be avoided. Self-interest played a role in the deliberations, as some moderates feared the loss of their wealth and station in the democratic aftermath of a revolution. One attempt at reconciliation with Britain was the so-called Olive Branch Petition of John Dickinson, imploring King George III to personally step in and oversee a settlement to the re-

cent troubles. Like many other American attempts at nego-
tiation, it fell on deaf ears.

In June 1775, George Washington was named commander in chief of the colonial forces. His appointment was
based on his previous military experience with the British
army in the Seven Years' War and his prominent place in the
Virginia establishment. The radical delegates from New England felt Washington was a good choice, as a southerner,
thereby encouraging the southern colonies to send troops to
the north to fight the British. Another attractive aspect of
Washington's character was his formidable personality (and
the fact that he insisted on taking the job without pay).

On the same day that Washington was commissioned as
the leader of the rebellious Americans, the first major battle
of the war took place in Boston. At the Battle of Bunker Hill
(which actually took place on Breed's Hill, closer to Boston),
colonial troops held the high ground and repelled the British
until the third assault. The British suffered terribly, with
1,054 casualties; the Americans lost 400 killed or captured.
This first battle of the American Revolution would prove to
be the bloodiest in the war.

'Tis Time to Part

The Second Continental Congress was slow to break ties
with the British Empire. With full-scale war just hundreds of
miles away, moderates still controlled the floor. In January
1776, however, a pamphlet galvanized public opinion.
Thomas Paine, a recent British immigrant, wrote *Common
Sense*, a forceful call for independence. To Paine, it was common sense that King George III was to blame for Americans'
troubles, and independence was the only solution. Paine put
it succinctly: "The blood of the slain, the weeping voice of
nature cries, ''TIS TIME TO PART.'"

The strong public support of Paine's message swayed the
Continental Congress toward freedom. On June 7, 1776,
Richard Henry Lee, one of the most outspoken delegates,
called for the colonies to be "free and independent states" and
the connections between Britain and the American colonies
to be "totally dissolved." The congress assigned the task of

formally presenting a statement of intentions to another Virginian, Thomas Jefferson, and to Benjamin Franklin and John Adams. Jefferson is credited with the actual writing of the Declaration of Independence, formally ratified on July 4. With its signing the former colonies of British North America became free and independent states.

In the world outside the halls of congress, however, the British were going to war. British forces were augmented by more than thirty thousand German soldiers, called Hessians, and other British subjects forced into service. In June and July of 1776, the British brought an immense flotilla of ships into New York harbor with thirty battleships, more than forty thousand men, and three hundred supply ships. Colonial leaders, including Washington, knew that these forces would overwhelm the smaller Continental Army, and quietly withdrew the American troops. Had the British been able to engage the Americans in New York, the war would have been over. As it was, the British would never again be so close to ending the war in their favor.

In September 1776, Americans John Adams and Benjamin Franklin met with British admiral Lord Richard Howe for a peace conference on Staten Island in New York. Howe insisted that the colonists revoke the Declaration of Independence, an impossible demand to the two American negotiators. Later in the month the congress appointed Thomas Jefferson, Franklin, and Silas Deene to negotiate treaties with other European nations, seeking either military and financial aid or assurances that the Europeans would not enter the war on the British side.

"The Summer Soldier and the Sunshine Patriot"

By the winter of 1776, the Continental Army was hard pressed to point to a recent victory in the field. Washington's forces had been in retreat to Philadelphia for four months and newly formed naval forces had been decimated in October. The congress abandoned Philadelphia, fearing a battle, and moved south to Baltimore. The Americans needed a victory to lift flagging morale. Washington conceived a bold plan to split his forces and recross the Delaware River, his goal the British outposts in New Jersey. With only a third of his forces, Washington stunned the British, capturing more than one thousand Hessians and defeating British forces at Trenton and Princeton.

Washington lost most of his troops over the next few months, however; historians Tindall and Shi describe the winter in Morristown:

> Washington's army nearly disintegrated as enlistments expired and deserters fled. . . . Only about 1000 soldiers stuck it out. With the spring thaw, however, recruits began to arrive to claim the bounty of $20 and 100 acres of land offered by Congress for those who would enlist for three years.[8]

By the middle of the spring of 1777, Washington had nine thousand soldiers to command and renewed the fighting in the northern colonies. John Paul Jones secured naval victories along the English coast in 1778, and Americans began to believe the war might be won.

A True World War

In 1777 the efforts of the American ambassadors in Europe began to bear results. The French, longtime rivals of the British in Europe and North America, pledged their unofficial assistance to the American cause. In July 1777, the marquis de Lafayette, a nineteen-year-old French aristocrat, offered his assistance to George Washington, without pay. Washington made him a trusted adviser and major general in the Continental Army. Throughout the year, American forces made inroads, with a major victory at Saratoga.

In November 1777, the congress adopted the Articles of Confederation for the establishment of a government for the new United States of America, with the congress as sole authority. With a governmental structure in place, the United States negotiated formal treaties with the French government. In February 1778, the United States and France signed the Treaty of Amity and Commerce and the Treaty of Alliance. These treaties stated that France officially recognized the United States as an independent nation and that the two nations would fight against the British until independence was achieved. Historian Alexander Deconde described the importance of the alliance:

> At last, as Americans had hoped and assumed it would, the French alliance transformed their Revolution . . . into a key element in an international war. Later, Spain and the Netherlands also fought against England. . . . The alliance proved the essential element or "deciding factor." Diplomatic historians appear to consider this judgment virtually as dogma; few depart from it. Without the alliance, they say, the Revolution would have failed.[9]

With other European nations on the side of the Americans, Britain now was surrounded by foes. Dutch, French, and Spanish ships joined Americans in harassing the British navy, and Britain was concerned that while the majority of its forces were engaged in America, it was vulnerable to attack at home.

In March 1778 the British offered to sign a peace treaty with the Americans agreeing to all of the original colonial demands but denying the colonies independence. These terms might have swayed the congress three years earlier, but the spirit of freedom was running wild in the United States; the offer was rejected and the war continued.

The British had expected to win the war in less than a year. Now, three years later, morale in the British ranks was ebbing. European support of the Americans and the hard stand of the congress gave many British subjects pause: Should they continue this bloody conflict? Meanwhile, the United States was poised to gain the edge it needed in the final phase of the American Revolution: the southern campaigns.

The Final Years of Bloodshed

By 1779, though the leadership of the new United States was behind the independence movement, the people were becoming weary of the war. The British, perhaps sensing hesitancy in the population, decided to strike forcefully at the South. But the British policy of destroying the southern infrastructure and economy, though effective, inspired southerners' desire for independence beyond that felt in 1776.

The British won conventional victories at Savannah and Charleston, but American patriots continually harassed their forces as they moved through the countryside. One of these patriots, Francis Marion, alias Swamp Fox, was extremely successful at toying with the British troops through raids and sabotage. Men who might already have had enough fighting were dogged by Marion's men and possibly made more susceptible to mistakes.

Washington sent his ablest general, Nathanael Greene, to oversee the troop movements of the American regulars. Greene realized the effects of quick strikes and innovative tactics on the British and employed them to confound General Charles Cornwallis of the British army. Cornwallis was ordered to fall back to a defensible position and hold his ground. Cornwallis, confident his choice was wise, moved his troops to Yorktown and began to construct earthen mounds as fortifications.

The World Turn'd Upside Down

As Cornwallis fell back, French and American troops gathered to make a final push against the British. They saw their opportunity as Cornwallis had concentrated his troops and organized an all-out attack on his position at Yorktown. Washington and the count de Rochambeau met Lafayette in Virginia and moved their combined forces into position. A French fleet under Admiral de Grasse moved into the York River to pin the British troops down without the possibility of reinforcements.

Washington finally held a numerical superiority over the British in a major battle. With a combined army of seventeen thousand men under his command and French cannons firing on British positions, Washington laid siege to Yorktown from September 28 to the middle of October. Cornwallis realized his dire situation and surrendered his entire army, more than nine thousand men, to the Americans on October 17, 1781. As the formal surrender was drawn up two days later, a British military band played the old tune "The World Turn'd Upside Down," a fitting description of British hopes in North America.

The devastating defeat of Cornwallis at Yorktown brought sharp calls for peace in the halls of Parliament. The overall cost of the war and the now obvious resolve of the American people had turned the hearts of many of the British people. As the British forces were being withdrawn from North America, the House of Commons voted against continuing the war in America. By March 1782, Parliament had empowered the king to negotiate peace with the United States. Many Loyalists fled the former colonies to New Brunswick and Nova Scotia, abandoning their property to those who remained.

Lord North, who had held his position throughout the war, resigned and a new commission headed by the duke of Rockingham took control. Rockingham was known to be sympathetic to the American cause, and had in fact brought about the repeal of the Stamp Act. Rockingham died in September 1782, replaced by Lord Shelburne as chief minister; Shelburne directed the Paris negotiations.

The United States sent its most accomplished statesmen— John Adams, Benjamin Franklin, John Jay, and Henry Laurens—to the peace conference. Immediately they faced the complications of the earlier treaty with France and France's promises to Spain. The United States was bound to fight Britain until France made peace, and the French had pledged to help the Spanish recover Gibraltar, a military outpost at the mouth of the Mediterranean Sea. Jay and Franklin were not optimistic that Britain would voluntarily give up such a strategic spot and decided to strike a separate peace with the British, without informing the French. When the terms of this agreement were presented to France and Spain, their representatives realized that the war for Gibraltar was not a part of the American Revolution. Through 1783, the European nations and the United States negotiated terms, and the Treaty of Paris was signed on September 3, 1783.

The End of the War

In the Treaty of Paris, Great Britain recognized the independence of the United States and agreed that the Mississippi was the western boundary of its ceded territory. The northern and southern boundaries were still in dispute. The

British "gave" the Americans the right to fish off the New England coast and promised to resolve issues of British mercantile debt to American firms. And with that, the domination of the British Empire over the United States of America ended. But the problems of the United states had just begun.

John Adams described the American Revolution not as a military battle between the British and the Americans, but a shift in political views:

> The Revolution was effected before the war commenced. The Revolution was in the minds and hearts of the people. . . . This radical change in the principles, opinions, sentiments, and affections of the people, was the real American Revolution.[10]

Adams was correct in that the military battles were less significant then the social and political changes that occurred in the 1770s and 1780s. The colonies had gone from subjects of the British Empire to independent colonies to part of United States under the Articles of Confederation. As the era of postwar governance dawned, the leaders of America came to realize that the Articles of Confederation had been effective during the Revolution but were inadequate to administer a country still unresolved regarding states' versus federal powers.

The move to modify the Articles of Confederation started as soon as the war was over. The debate between those who wanted more power allotted to the individual states and those who wanted a strong central government led to the formation of the Constitution. Meanwhile, other issues such as the payment of war debts and foreign policy came to the fore.

Another pressing issue concerned the interpretation of the principle that started the Revolution in the first place: liberty. How could the United States deny equality to groups who had participated in the war (i.e., women, Native Americans and blacks) while expressing the ideal of equality for all?

The long-term effects of the American Revolution were felt not only in North America but throughout the world. In 1789 the French Revolution abolished the monarchy and advanced democratic principles. However, the government structures that resulted in France were short lived. The American Revolution, born of the best minds and political strategists of its age, produced a government and political institutions that have endured for more than two hundred years.

Americans would grapple with the unanswered questions of the Revolution, those of equality and states' rights versus federal rights, for centuries.

Notes

1. R.R. Palmer, *The Age of Democratic Revolution: The Challenge*. Princeton, NJ: Princeton University Press, 1959.

2. The prohibition on printing paper money had first been imposed in New England in 1751; the 1764 act extended the prohibition to all the colonies.

3. James Otis, *The Rights of British Colonies, Asserted and Proved*. Boston: Edes and Gill, 1764.

4. Pauline Maier, *From Resistance to Revolution: Colonial Radicals and the Development of American Opposition to Britain*. New York: Knopf, 1972.

5. Norman K. Risjord, *Forging the American Republic, 1760–1815*. Reading, MA: Addison-Wesley, 1973.

6. George Brown Tindall and David E. Shi, *America: A Narrative History*. New York: W.W. Norton, 1989.

7. Quoted in Milton Meltzer, *The American Revolutionaries: A History in Their Own Words, 1750–1800*. New York: Thomas Crowell, 1987.

8. Tindall and Shi, *America*, 127.

9. Alexander Deconde, "The French Alliance in Historical Speculation," in *Diplomacy and Revolution: The Franco-American Alliance of 1778*, Ronald Hoffman and Peter J. Albert, eds. Charlottesville: University Press of Virginia, 1981.

10. Quoted in Tindall and Shi, 140.

Chapter 1

The Years Before: The Causes of the American Revolution

Turning | Points
IN WORLD HISTORY

Economics Drove the American Revolution

James A. Henretta and Gregory H. Nobles

James A. Henretta and Gregory H. Nobles are authorities on the economies of the American colonies. Both admit that social change contributed to the revolutionary movement, but maintain that economic factors weighed much more heavily on the minds of American colonists. For the authors, and for the colonists in their examples, taxation without representation incited revolutionary zeal, not a thirst for equality for all. Henretta is the Priscilla Alden Burke Professor of American History at the University of Maryland. Nobles is chair of the History, Technology, and Society Department at Georgia Tech University.

The origins of the American War of Independence are numerous and tangled. In retrospect, it is clear that several critical preconditions for a successful movement for self-determination had been fulfilled by 1765. First, an experienced and self-confident group of political leaders had appeared in most colonies. They controlled representative institutions that enjoyed broad support among the white population. Second, three generations of rapid demographic change and economic growth had resulted in a prosperous agricultural and commercial system. Finally, changes in family life, religious practice, ethnic composition, and social authority had weakened traditional habits of political deference.

Although these social changes were prerequisites for rebellion, they were not by themselves a sufficient cause. A further set of preconditions stemmed from the French and Indian War. The war prompted an unsettling economic cycle of prosperity and recession in America. In addition, it engendered new cultural tensions. Arrogant British officers treated American "provincials" or "peasants" (as they often called them) with contempt, which led to widespread suspicion of imperial motives and policies. The war also increased the British national debt from £75 million to £133 million, setting off motions in Parliament that the prosperous colonists should shoulder part of this economic burden. Yet even these dangerously disruptive forces did not, in themselves, lead inescapably toward political violence.

The American independence movement developed finally in direct response to a third set of causes—new British measures of taxation and control. These "immediate" causes also had their origins in Britain's recent war with France. . . .

Once the French and Indian War had confirmed British mastery over trade with Asia, Africa, and Spanish America, the American settlements themselves would have to be brought under firm control. . . .

In 1762, Parliament passed a new revenue act that reformed the customs service. This act eliminated "absentee" officials who lived in England and received payments from easily corruptible deputies in the colonies. The ministry also directed the Royal Navy to apprehend smugglers. . . .

The Sugar Act and the Stamp Act

Other British actions had equally profound psychological and financial effects. Just as the revitalized customs service began to drain much needed specie from the American economy, Parliament enacted the Currency Act of 1764. This legislation prohibited colonial assemblies from printing paper money to use as legal tender. The colonists could no longer issue currency to provide an adequate supply of money or to stimulate business activity.

Another revenue act, the Sugar Act of 1764, likewise threatened American economic interests. The act lowered the import duty on molasses produced in the French West Indies from 6 pence to 3 pence per gallon. However, to ensure the collection of this duty, the act expanded the jurisdiction of the vice-admiralty courts. Since these courts were administrative tribunals in which judges sat alone, without juries, merchants could no longer depend on sympathetic juries of colonists to acquit them of smuggling charges. "What has America done," asked the author of one pamphlet, "to be disfranchised and stripped of so invaluable a privilege as the trial by jury?"

The British government also made other crucial changes in the American legal system. The Sugar Act transferred the burden of proof from customs officials to accused merchants, who now had to demonstrate that their trade was legal under the Navigation Acts. The Sugar Act also gave officials the authority to seize cargoes if there was the slightest "probable cause" that they were contraband, thus preempting merchants' potential suits for false arrest. Finally, the ministry instructed royal governors to issue new commissions to all colonial judges. Henceforth, judges in America would no longer hold office for life or even during "good behavior" but would serve only "at the pleasure of the crown." Lawyers in New York and South Carolina claimed this limited judicial tenure violated their "liberties and privileges" as Englishmen, but their protests were to no avail. Through a series of dramatic legal initiatives, the British Crown and Parliament had imposed new economic restrictions on the continental colonies and altered the character of their judicial systems. . . .

Parliament's passage of the Stamp Act of 1765 brought these constitutional issues to the forefront. Like the Sugar Act, the new legislation was the brainchild of George Grenville, the British prime minister. Similar taxes had been collected in England since 1694; by the 1760s these taxes raised £300,000 in revenue each year. Grenville hoped to raise a similar amount in America. His legislation required the colonists to buy tax stamps from royal collectors and to affix them to a wide variety of printed materials and legal documents. Moreover, the stamps had to be paid for in sterling (rather than with colonial currency), and the law would be enforced by the vice-admiralty courts (rather than colonial common law juries).

Grenville imposed this direct tax for two reasons. First, he wanted the colonists to defray some of the costs of defending the empire. The Stamp Act specifically stated that its proceeds were to be used to pay royal officials and the British troops guarding the American frontier. Second, and perhaps more important, Grenville was determined to assert British sovereignty over the colonies and their power-hungry representative assemblies. And he wanted to do so in a way that penetrated into the very heart of colonial society. The new stamps would appear on every newspaper, book, and almanac, on every legal document and bill of lading, and

---

Resisting the British

While early actions of the British were taken against the city of Boston, some colonists wanted to show that these were actually actions against all of the colonies. Here, a member of Boston's Committee of Correspondence tried to use the blocking of Boston harbor as a rallying point for other colonial leaders.

GENTLEMEN: With mingled concern and indignation, the Committee of Correspondence for this town have seen an Act for blocking up the harbour of *Boston*.

Rome designing to destroy the city of *Carthage*, barbarously required of the *Carthagenians* that they should forsake their city, and remove their habitations twelve miles from the sea. The consideration of the inveterate hatred occasioned by the long and bloody wars which had subsisted between *Rome* and *Carthage*; the remembrance of several hundred thousand *Romans* killed in those wars, and several hundred towns plundered by the *Carthagenians*, are some excuse for the *Roman* severity; but the cruel and unnatural treatment which the town of *Boston* has received from *Great Britain*, will admit of no palliation. The metropolis of a most affectionate and loyal Colony, which in all the wars of *Great Britain* hath gloriously supported the *British* interest in *America*, and even by their wise and vigorous efforts made a conquest which gave peace to *Europe*, is now threatened with destruction, for no other cause, but because the people have bravely determined not to become slaves.

We have long felt for the town of *Boston*; we heartily sympa-

on the liquor licenses and playing cards in every tavern. This symbol of imperial authority would be everywhere and would be enforced by British-controlled courts as a constant testimony to the supremacy of Parliament. Grenville's goals found a broad base of support among members of the British political elite. Despite appeals by American merchants and agents and their British associates, Parliament passed the Stamp Act by an overwhelming margin. . . .

In nearly every major seaport, British authority was challenged and found lacking. Only in a few places, such as

thize with our brethren upon this alarming occasion; we are much pleased with the noble firmness with which this cruel edict is received in *Boston*. We highly approve the measures taken by the town, and are entirely of opinion that the joint resolution of the Colonies to stop all importations from and exportations to *Great Britain* and the *West Indies*, until the Act is repeled, will infallibly produce the desired effect.

The country which we possess, blessed be *God!* affords every necessary of life. We are morally certain, that with the common blessings of Heaven upon our industry and frugality, we can live comfortably, without importing a single article from *Britain* or the *West Indies*; and we are equally certain, that neither *England* nor the *West Indies* can subsist long without us; their own preservation therefore, will compel them to do us justice.

This horrid attack upon the town of *Boston*, we consider not as an attempt upon that town singly, but upon the whole Continent. We are therefore determined to use our whole influence for the support of the town of *Boston*, in the same manner as if the attack had been made on the metropolis of this Colony; and we doubt not but the other Colonies will consider this arbitrary and tyrannical edict in the same light, and heartily unite with the friends of liberty in *Boston* in support of the common cause.

That infinite wisdom may direct and preserve all the Colonies, is the ardent prayer of, &c., &c.

Stanley I. Kutler, *Looking for America: The People's History*. Vol. 1. New York: W.W. Norton and Company, 1979.

Philadelphia, was there sufficient local support to shore up the crumbling facade of imperial law and order. The ship carpenters who belonged to two organizations, the White Oaks and the Hearts of Oak, were longstanding supporters of Benjamin Franklin. Forming an "Association for the Preservation of the Peace," they prevented the Sons of Liberty from destroying the house of John Hughes, Franklin's associate and the newly appointed tax collector.

The crisis over the Stamp Act exposed the weakness of British power in America. For decades, colonial political leaders had challenged specific powers and actions of royal governors, but they had not questioned the legitimacy of the political system. Many wealthy merchants and influential artisans now directly repudiated imperial tax legislation. Along with journeymen and sailors, they joined in extralegal crowd actions aimed against British authorities and their colonial supporters. . . .

Opposition to the Stamp Act

Popular mobilization threatened the power of all members of the ruling elite, whether British or American. Some artisans and farmers refused to defer to traditional leaders; they wanted greater political influence for their social groups. General Thomas Gage reported that New York merchants were now "terrified at the Spirit they had raised" and worried that "popular Fury was not to be guided." Indeed, an anonymous pamphleteer in New York City advanced the radical proposition that ultimate political authority rested in the popular will. "To overthrow [the Stamp Act]," he proclaimed, "nothing is wanted but your own Resolution, for great is the Authority and Power of the People." In the end, the Stamp Act created a crisis of authority both in the British empire and in the traditional American political system. . . .

To oppose the Stamp Act, most colonial assemblies sent representatives to an extralegal congress in New York City in December, 1765. American political leaders, along with merchants, met to exchange information and ideas about imperial policy. The congress began a new stage in American political development. Previously each assembly had dealt on an individual basis with ministers and bureaucrats in London. Elected colonial officials had convened only once—in Albany, New York, in 1754, to discuss military co-operation against France. When the Stamp Act congress convened in December, 1765, the delegates humbly acknowledged "all due subordination" to Parliament and asked for repeal of the act. Not so humbly, they asserted that "no taxes ever have been, or can be constitutionally imposed on them, but by their respective legislatures."

American public opinion was far in advance of the sentiments of most delegates to the congress. New popular leaders, such as Samuel Adams and Patrick Henry, strongly endorsed both mob resistance and a complete boycott of all British manufactured goods. The Non-Importation Agreement subscribed to by American merchants in 1765 appealed to various colonial groups and interests. Political leaders—men familiar with the pragmatic world of power—praised the agreement's realistic approach; they felt that a successful boycott would force Parliament to respect American rights. Many Sons of Liberty also supported the agreement. As artisans who manufactured boots, sailcloth, rope, and tinware, they welcomed the boycott of the low-priced imports that competed with their products. Ministers and moralists also praised the boycott as a remedy for the disease of overconsumption that was eating away at the spiritual health of American society.

Finally, the merchant community actively supported non-importation. Many merchants had imported huge stocks of British textiles, ceramics, and other goods in 1763 and 1764, before the postwar recession cut sales. The Non-Importation Agreement allowed them to protest against British taxes and regulations while reducing their excess inventories. "We are well convinced something of this sort is absolutely necessary at this time," Philadelphia merchant John Chew wrote to an associate in November, 1765, "from the great much too large importation that has for sometime past been made. There will be no wanted goods for a twelve month.". . .

Many politically aware Americans began to look with suspicion on all British mercantile regulations. For them, these laws had become a system of economic imperialism. They accused British merchants, manufacturers, and politicians of using their superior financial resources to exploit the relatively undeveloped colonies. One radical New York City pamphleteer condemned those Americans who protested only against direct taxation. "They have on the whole rather betrayed than defended the cause . . . ," he charged, for "tho' they condemn the Stamp-Act, [they] would have us at the mercy of the British Parliament in every article but taxation.". . .

Strong Anti-British Feelings Erupt

A strong wave of anti-British and nationalist sentiment swept across the colonies. Like most expressions of the popular will, these outbursts were not totally spontaneous. They were the final products of a decade of imperial crisis and of years of patient organization. Since 1768, Patriots had used their "Committees of Correspondence" to mobilize support in farming regions. This political agitation was about to pay off. Distressed by the terms of the Massachusetts Government Act, the colony's farmers rose in rebellion. In Worcester, militia companies ousted their old officers and appointed men who repudiated the authority of the newly appointed military governor, Thomas Gage. Armed farmers gathered on the village green, prevented the opening of the regular law courts, and forced royally appointed judges to resign their posts. The Worcester County Committees of Correspondence proposed a "convention of the people"; it would "devise proper ways and means" to create new institutions of government in Massachusetts.

Patriots in other colonies similarly repudiated British authority. In September, 1774, the gentlemen and freeholders of Fairfax County, Virginia, formed an "independent Company of Voluntiers" for "learning & practising the military Exercise & Discipline." Soon they broadened the militia training to include "all the able-bodied Freemen from eighteen to fifty Years of Age." Poorer volunteers would "form a Company of Marksmen . . . distinguishing [their] Dress . . . by painted Hunting-Shirts and Indian Boots." In Philadelphia, Scotch-Irish and German artisans took control of the city's political organizations from Quaker and Anglican merchants. They demanded support for a new pact of nonimportation to force the repeal of the Coercive Acts. . . .

The First Continental Congress met in Philadelphia in the autumn of 1774. John Dickinson and Joseph Galloway of Pennsylvania rallied "men of loyal principles" behind a final attempt at reconciliation. To resolve the constitutional deadlock, Galloway proposed a new system of imperial authority. His plan called for the king to appoint a governor-general over all of the colonies and for the British Parliament to grant powers of legislation and taxation to a representative American parliament.

Dickinson and Galloway found substantial support for this proposal among delegates from the middle colonies. The diversity of social groups and political interests in Pennsylvania, New York, and New Jersey had accustomed leaders in those colonies to explore compromise solutions. The two Pennsylvanians also sought allies among the Virginia delegation, whose members feared "the low, levelling principles" of the radical Patriots from Massachusetts. However, because of the severity of the Coercive Acts, the southern delegates were even more suspicious of British intentions. They heeded the emotional warnings of the representatives from New England. By the margin of a single vote, the delegates rejected Galloway's plan. Patriot forces in the Continental Congress then secured the passage of resolutions calling for the nonimportation of British goods and threatening to stop American exports as well. Finally, the delegates attacked the Declaratory Act and other British legislation affecting the "life, liberty, [and] property" of Americans as "unconstitutional, dangerous and destructive.". . .

A majority of politically active Americans had already declared their allegiance. By the end of 1774, the Patriots' control of the countryside vastly reduced the authority of the royal governors. General Thomas Gage, the newly appointed military governor of Massachusetts, actually exercised power only in Boston. In the spring of 1775, the British government ordered Gage to suppress the illegal Patriot assembly, which was meeting in nearby Concord, and to capture its leaders and its stores of ammunition and supplies. For the first time in the decade-long confrontation, the imperial authorities ordered the use of armed force. The Patriots were equally prepared for violence. Dozens of militia companies stood ready to take up arms "at a minute's notice." On April 19, these "Minutemen" met Gage's troops at Lexington and Concord. The Patriot soldiers inflicted heavy casualties on the British troops as they retreated back to Boston.

In the ten years since the Stamp Act crisis, the colonists had moved from verbal resistance to armed rebellion. At first, Americans had simply defended their traditional privileges within the British empire. The debate over taxation led them onto new constitutional and political ground. American political leaders drew upon the Whig and Country Party ideology to justify their opposition to the new policies of economic and political imperialism. The force of events prompted the colonists to define their self-interests as members of distinct social groups and as residents of America. By 1775, the possibility of reconciliation with Great Britain was slim.

Britain's Lack of Diplomacy Led to Revolution

John Richard Alden

The impetus for the American Revolution is one of the most thoroughly studied subjects in American history. One factor cannot be ignored; the antagonistic relationship between the British Parliament and several of the American colonies. Historian John Richard Alden discusses the relationship between the government of the British Empire and the colonial revolutionaries of the mid-1700s. Alden contends that the British Parliament's greatest blunder was its desire to bring the colonies back into the empire by force, instead of diplomacy and cooperation. Alden was a professor of history at the University of Nebraska and at Duke University in Durham, North Carolina.

At the middle of the third quarter of the eighteenth century Britain was the greatest of the great European powers. Triumphant on land and sea in the Seven Years' War then ending, she reigned over all the wide waters frequently traversed by Europeans and over a vast and growing empire. In the year 1763 no European navy, perhaps no combination of two European navies, could successfully challenge her fleets and her sailors. Gibraltar and Minorca, the keys to the western Mediterranean, were British properties; she dominated Bombay, Madras, and Bengal in India, and could reasonably expect to develop and to exploit the resources of that subcontinent without molestation from Europeans; small but valuable colonies on the west coast of Africa were hers; she had obtained lucrative economic privileges, if not territorial rights, on the coasts of Nicaragua and Honduras; and the

Excerpted from *The American Revolution, 1775–1783*, by John R. Alden. Copyright ©1954 by Harper & Brothers. Copyright renewed. Reprinted by permission of HarperCollins Publishers, Inc.

British flag flew over the Bermudas, the Bahamas, Jamaica, Barbados, and other West Indian islands. On the mainland of North America British territory extended from the Atlantic to the Mississippi and from the Gulf of Mexico to the Arctic Ocean. British merchant shipping had outstripped all competitors; British commerce was by the standards of the time immense and profitable; having coal and iron, Britain was already making progress in the Industrial Revolution, well in advance of her European rivals. Continental rulers and peoples looked across the narrow seas for leadership.

By 1783 Britain had lost the bulk of her North American possessions, her most prized colonies. Having exhibited peculiar genius for empire-building, Britain was, astonishingly, the first of the great powers to be forced to acknowledge the political independence of colonials. The entrance into the contentious family of nations of the United States of America, formed from the very heart of the British Empire, was an event that few Europeans would have anticipated a generation earlier. Almost equally surprising was the fact that the newcomer came not in the trappings of monarchy but in the form of a republic, with institutions and ideals pointing toward political and social democracy. Hence, it was entirely fitting that, in the ceremonies accompanying the surrender of Lord Cornwallis, British musicians played "The World Turned Upside Down."

Europeans Aided the Colonists

This sudden reversal in the fortunes of Britain and the rapid birth of the United States are attributable at least in a measure to antagonisms existing between Britain and several European states. It is not at all inconceivable that the Americans would have won their independence without either foreign allies or foreign aid of any sort. Yet European money and munitions and the entrance of France and Spain into the war of the American Revolution undoubtedly hastened, if they did not assure, British defeat and American victory. The intervention of the Bourbon kingdoms and of other states in the struggle was prompted hardly at all by sympathy with the Americans, but rather by the opportunity to strike at hated Britain and to profit from her difficulties. In her rise to wealth and dominance Britain had trampled upon the ambitions of her rivals, Holland, Spain, and France. Viewed after 1763 as a mortal enemy at the courts of Versailles and Madrid, Britain made no move to placate her foes and failed to build alliances with the states of central and eastern Europe which might have gained for her powerful friends in time of need.

These abrupt changes must also be ascribed in some degree to British remissness with respect to land and naval forces. Although the traditionally small army was somewhat larger after 1763 than it was before the Seven Years' War, its duties were far greater than before the conflict. Denuding the garrison forces in the home islands, Britain could not put fifteen thousand redcoats in the field in America in 1775. Britain's wooden walls were also neglected. In the day of danger, thanks in some part to the incompetence of the Earl of Sandwich, in larger degree to a desire to economize, the fleet was no more than equal to that of France. Neglected and ill-equipped, His Majesty's ships in 1775 were frequently old, and at least some were rotten with age. Meanwhile France had reconstructed her navy. Britain would pay heavily in consequence and would be in jeopardy as she had not been since the sailing of the Spanish Armada.

Internal Conflict

Inadequate in diplomacy and indifferent to the armed services during the period 1763–75, Britain during the same span was also weakened by corruption and civil commotion. Morality in public affairs was at low ebb at the close of the Seven Years' War. It did not rise, perhaps sank still further, as George III purchased support in order to restore the royal power. Grievous though the results of bribery by the King were upon British public character, his long campaign to reestablish monarchical authority produced other and greater evils. A core of politicians seduced by cash and position came in increasing numbers to occupy Cabinet seats and other posts of authority, especially after 1767. Beyond the fact that they could be counted on to do the King's bidding, they seldom had marked qualifications for office. Nor was their master sufficiently gifted to compensate for their defects. Moreover, although George III was able during several critical years to influence and eventually to dominate both Cabinet and Parliament, there were those whom he would not and perhaps a handful whom he could not cajole or buy. As his purpose to rule as well as reign became evident, bitter opposition sprang up. Many enemies of the King would have been content to reduce the authority of George III to the proportions of that exercised by George II; others, especially after open fighting had begun in America, desired also to take further moderate steps toward political democracy. There were in Britain a very few who wished for a republic.

Patrick Henry's Official Protest

The colonies rejoiced in the rise of parliamentary power until that power was turned against them. Patrick Henry's address to the Virginia Assembly gave voice to the issues that galvanized many Americans in the 1760s.

[1.] Resolved: That the first adventurers and settlers of this His Majesty's [George III] colony and dominion brought with them, and transmitted to their posterity . . . all the privileges, franchises, and immunities that have at any time been held, enjoyed, and possessed by the people of Great Britain.

[2.] Resolved: That by two royal charters, granted by King James the First, the colonists aforesaid are declared entitled to all the privileges, liberties, and immunities of denizens and natural-born subjects, to all intents and purposes as if they had been abiding and born within the realm of England.

[3.] Resolved: That the taxation of the people by themselves, or by persons chosen by themselves to represent them, who [can] only know what taxes the people are able to bear, and the easiest mode of raising them, and are equally affected by such taxes themselves, is the distinguishing characteristic of British freedom, and without which the ancient Constitution cannot subsist.

[4.] Resolved: That his Majesty's liege people of this most

Divided among themselves, the opponents of the monarch and his associates were unable to gain control of the House of Commons and the Cabinet during the fateful years 1770–82. Nevertheless, they were numerous, and Britain was seriously torn by domestic discord when unity was desirable for the defense of the home islands and almost indispensable to the preservation of the empire. Indeed, some of the enemies of the King in Britain looked upon the Americans who rose against the British government after 1763 as political allies, and even came to identify them, perhaps mistakenly, with their own cause.

Above all, the swift rending of the British Empire and the appearance of the American Union are to be explained by

---

ancient colony have uninterruptedly enjoyed the right of being thus governed by their own Assembly in the article of their taxes and internal police, and that the same hath never been forfeited . . . but hath been constantly recognized by the kings and people of Great Britain.

[5.] Resolved, therefore: That the General Assembly of this colony have the only and sole exclusive right and power to lay taxes . . . upon the inhabitants of this colony, and that every attempt to vest such power in any person or persons whatsoever, other than the General Assembly aforesaid, has a manifest tendency to destroy British [as] well as American freedom.

[6.] Resolved: That his Majesty's liege people, the inhabitants of this colony, are not bound to yield obedience to any law or ordinance whatever designed to impose any taxation whatsoever upon them, other than the laws or ordinances of the General Assembly aforesaid.

[7.] Resolved: That any person who shall by speaking or writing, assert or maintain that any person or persons, other than the General Assembly of this colony, have any right or power to impose or lay any taxation on the people here, shall be deemed an enemy to his Majesty's colony.

From Milton Meltzer, ed., *The American Revolutionaries: A History in Their Own Words, 1750–1800*. New York: Thomas Y. Crowell, 1987.

the mistakes of the British government in dealing with the American colonies after 1763, blunders which drove them into armed rebellion. For generations the inhabitants of these maturing colonies had been moving in the direction of home rule. After the close of the Seven Years' War, George Grenville, Charles Townshend, Lord North, the Earl of Hillsborough, George III, and others who wielded power attempted to stem, and even to reverse, this tide. They also tried, for the first time in the history of the mainland colonies, to extract from them a large revenue through taxation levied by Parliament. . . .

In the winter of 1774–75 the British government learned that America had become a powder keg. Blame for this situation must be attributed in far larger measure to the inadequacies of George III and British politicians than to the activities of the radical leadership in America. Failure of the British supporters of the post-1763 policy to sustain their program over the objections of those who urged conciliation produced vacillations between harshness and weakness which, in turn, stiffened or invited American resistance. Had the new policy been firmly and steadily pushed in the Stamp Act crisis, it is barely possible that American resistance might have been peacefully overcome. But wiser by far than a consistent course of coercion would have been the abandoning of the effort to turn back the colonial clock. An American policy based upon recognition of the maturity of the colonies and of their value to the mother country, together with an attitude of good will, might have postponed indefinitely the era of American independence. Neither George III nor any Cabinet member had ever been in America; they did not know the strength and spirit of the colonies, were unaware that they could not permanently be kept within the empire except upon their own terms.

Hence, the greatest blunder of the King, the Cabinet, and Parliament was their decision in 1775 to bring America to heel by armed might. In the final analysis George III himself was personally responsible for this decision. The dominance which he had gained in London and his limited understanding now involved Britain in a military conflict which she might well lose and one from which she was unlikely to gain enduring benefits through victory. With Europe as a whole hostile or coldly neutral, with a weakened navy, with a small army, with a large part of the people of the home island opposed to governmental policy, with Ireland restless, George III and his followers sought to conquer a colonial people in considerable part of English stock, separated from the home islands by a broad ocean. Moreover, in order to compel submission, they undertook to invade and to occupy the colonies. The extent of their folly was not generally known in Britain until France aligned herself with the Americans and the War of Independence widened into a struggle waged on four continents and their adjoining seas. However, shrewd British observers realized in 1775, and earlier, that the colonies, even without assistance from Europe, would not easily be overrun by British arms, and that it might prove impossible to break down their resistance.

The colonies lay three thousand miles beyond the Atlantic. The voyage across it required a month under the most favorable conditions and might consume two, three, and even four months. The distance and the smallness of sailing vessels created major difficulties in communications, and especially in transport, since British troops could not be expected to "live off the country" indefinitely. It seemed doubtful that Britain could gather sufficient manpower to overwhelm the colonists, even with the aid of those loyal to the King, since the American population, about two and one-half millions, was more than one-quarter of that of Britain. Besides, there was no strategic center, in fact no strategic centers, in America, the capture of which would give Britain victory. Communications within the colonies were poor. Flat and open country where warfare could be carried on in the European style was not common; and woods, hills, and swamps suited for operations by irregulars and guerilla fighters were plentiful. Even the American climate, with its extremes in temperature, favored the colonials, inured to it. Certainly they would be able to feed themselves as well as large armed forces. They could even produce rifles, muskets, shot, and clothing—in fact, the bulk of the military equipment required to wage war effectively. True, they possessed no great store of liquid capital. But it was not at all certain that the British nation, carrying a heavy national debt, could bear the economic burden of a long contest; and there could be no assurance that the colonists would quickly succumb to British arms. To be sure, the colonists, in order to carry on the struggle, would be forced to unify thirteen jealous governments, but the centralized British governmental machinery was notoriously inefficient.

When France and then Spain joined the Americans as open and military enemies of Britain, the question whether or not the colonies would remain within the British Empire was then and there decided. Thereafter, thoughtful men in British public life, if not George III himself, recognized that the colonists must either keep their independence or be induced to return to the empire. A government under the control of the King could neither cajole nor concede, and the war continued to final patriot victory.

Whigs in America

G.H. Guttridge

In this selection, G.H. Guttridge establishes a connection between the British Whigs and the beginning of the revolutionary movement in the American colonies. Guttridge is known for his research into the Whig philosophy and Edmund Burke. While many British Whigs supported colonial independence, and many revolutionaries referred to British Whigs as their philosophical ancestors, their methods did not always coincide.

At precisely the time when England was undergoing a revival of acute political controversy, an urgent imperial problem clamored for attention. The outline of that problem is well known. The American colonies had grown up within a system designed to increase the maritime and commercial resources of the English state, without competing unduly with existing economic interests. For a hundred years that system had remained rigid while conditions in England and in America had greatly changed. The colonies were developing into communities with economic needs that were diversified and complicated far beyond the simple conception of western plantations producing the raw materials and exotic goods needed to supplement the more advanced economy of the mother country. A persistently unfavorable balance of trade and an increasing burden of debt bore witness to the need for reorganization of commercial policy, but little was done, even at the opportunity of 1763, to correct the shortcomings of a theoretically balanced empire. . . .

The trend of English constitutional development . . . could

Excerpted from G.H. Guttridge, *English Whiggism and the American Revolution* (Berkeley and Los Angeles: University of California Press, 1963). Reprinted by permission of the publisher.

not be reversed; and when George Grenville attempted to stiffen and enforce control, the colonists began to consider the entire basis of parliamentary regulation, which had hitherto been accepted almost universally in England and very widely in America. . . .

The policy of Grenville marked the culmination of a long process of political friction. In many of the colonies the assembly had come to demand full parliamentary status on the English model, thus raising the question of ultimate authority within the colony. The governor was often dependent upon his assembly for the means of carrying on his administration, and could rarely obtain a permanent civil list. Meanwhile in England parliament had attained virtual supremacy, and thereby assumed a relation to the colonial assemblies not unlike that of the Stuart kings to their parliaments. For long it had threatened to impose direct taxation if the assemblies should persist in their demands for control; the threat was at last fulfilled when Grenville embarked upon this new adventure with his revenue act designed to include the widest possible range of colonial interests. Whereas by his enforcement of commercial regulation Grenville had aroused the opposition of particular colonial merchants and had raised the question of parliamentary control of trade, now by the Stamp Act he opened several other fields of controversy. The broad scope of the act touched the pockets of merchants, lawyers, and journalists, and also involved a serious drain of currency. The principle of parliamentary taxation was itself a fertile source of speculation, leading to the related problem of the authority of parliament over the internal affairs of a colony. The spokesmen of America found it necessary to do some hard thinking on the nature of government and the status of colonies. . . .

The Question of Authority

The authority of parliament was the central issue of the American Revolution, and American claims were directed to justify resistance by limiting or denying that authority. The extent and nature of opposition varied with times and with persons, but not the goal of the attack. In England, however, parliamentary supremacy had become the accepted basis of political thinking, which whigs and tories of the new dispensation shared. George III and Rockingham met here on common ground. The supremacy of parliament had been a whig creation. Executive and legislative power had been merged in "the crown in parliament." The whig system of patronage had made ministers the agents of parliamentary authority, the universal validity of which the descendants of Walpole had no desire to impair since it formed the basis of their own aristocratic monopoly. George III had accepted the system, but had intervened to turn it to his own uses. No political leader was more insistent than he in upholding the full supremacy of parliament. The American challenge to this supremacy therefore found no response from either of the main combatants in the struggle for power, whigs or new tories. Only from the political heretics in England could the colonists win wholehearted support. . . .

While a few old tories might find themselves strangely associated with the colonists in their desire to see a monarchical power free from complete dependence on the will of parliament, there were others whose sympathies with America were less negative. An increasing number of radical thinkers rejected parliamentary supremacy, or at least the supremacy of the existing parliament, not to restore the king, but to elevate the people. Wilkes the politician, Price and Priestley the popular philosophers, and Cartwright the propagandist held different shades of disbelief in a supreme parliament, but all emphasized the sovereignty of the people and were not afraid to tamper with the constitution in order to restore its ancient purity. They tended therefore to regard the American claims as just and feasible. It is true that many radicals were not opposed in principle to the authority of a sovereign legislature, provided it were fully representative. Some might even go so far as to insist on the right to tax the colonies while at the same time demanding great changes in the structure of parliament. But, like all rebels against the existing order, the reformers began by attacking the complete authority of the institution they wished to reform, and this involved a presumptive sympathy with its other enemies.

It was to their interest to work together; and English radicals usually accepted the proffered hand, even if, as with Wilkes, their original enthusiasm for the American cause was not above suspicion.

In appealing to the constitutional rights of Englishmen against a parliament that had failed in its trust the reformers allied themselves not only with American whigs, but also with Chatham. Chatham's position in the American controversies is of special significance, and seems to have been more consistent than the harsh criticism of some historians would suggest. It recalls the early stages of resistance to the Stuarts, when attempts were made to restrain the king within the bounds of law. Chatham retained this belief in a fundamental law, embodied in the English constitution, and expressed by Magna Carta and the Bill of Rights. When the American whigs sought to restrain parliament with the same constitutional argument, he rejoiced that America had resisted. He appealed to the constitution against the House of Commons in the Middlesex election; he invoked it against Lord Mansfield's judgment denying to juries the power of determining libels; and he upheld it against the Declaratory Act, which plainly asserted the rival doctrine of parliamentary supremacy. Moreover, Chatham's proposals to admit the limitation of parliamentary authority over America might well have produced a solution of the colonial problem, even though based on outmoded or untenable theories of government. Backed by his own great reputation in the colonies, Chatham was more likely to succeed than any other English statesman. His vision, shared by Conway and Thomas Pownall, as well as by his immediate followers, was of a great empire in which the English parliament was willing to respect the limitation of its sovereignty. It is difficult to see the feasibility at this time of any other kind of home rule. . . .

Whigs at Home and Abroad

During these years of domestic crisis, it is impossible to separate whig policy toward America from that toward Wilkes and the radicals at home. In both controversies the whigs agreed that violence could not be justified, but that grievances existed in the invasion of established rights of civil and political liberty. Dowdeswell in 1768 refused to give up opposition merely because Mr. Otis might agree with him, and he proceeded to denounce the transfer of cases of treason from America to England, saying that crimes were local and should be tried locally—an argument which would appeal with equal force to the whig zealot and the tory country gentleman. Burke took a similar line in 1770. Only a few weeks before, he had attempted to excuse the violence of the City of London, whose remonstrance against the neglect of its petition concerning the Middlesex elections had spared neither king, ministers, nor parliament. The American disorders were another symptom of the same disease. "Whenever the people are aggrieved," he declared, "they will be violent"; but this did not mean that grievances should never be redressed, and he attacked the attempt "to introduce into the administration of our justice a martial police." The tendency of these attacks was to criticize the actual conduct of administration rather than to enter upon the finer points of the colonial relationship. "The folly of the administration," said Burke, "has tended step by step to lead America into confusion."

Almost at the time of publishing his *Thoughts on the Cause of the Present Discontents* Burke attempted a similar formulation of whig criticism in regard to American policy. On May 9, 1770, he moved for an inquiry into the causes of American disorders, and the theme of his address was the administrative incompetence of those responsible for colonial government. For three years, he said, the whig opposition had abstained from any vexatious proceedings or inquiries which might have obstructed the ministerial plan of operations. America could not be governed, or American affairs administered, in parliament. "The characteristic of parliament is to establish general laws, to give general powers and large grants of public money. It is the part of administration to use those powers with judgment, to employ the supplies with effect. . . . The trust is a great one; but it is a trust that is necessary." From this assumption he proceeded to indict the incompetence, the inconsistency, and the weakness of ministers, who had sent ill-judged and irreconcilable orders to colonial governors, had provided terrorizing legislation which was not carried into effect, and had pledged the faith of the crown for the future leniency of parliament. "His Majesty . . . is to receive all the thanks for removing public burdens; and parliament all the odium of laying them on. . . . All is shaken to the foundation by the entire absence of common sense.

In thus founding their American policy upon administrative responsibility rather than raise the basic problem of authority, the whigs tacitly recognized the fact that they were in a difficult position. They would not join Chatham in restricting the supremacy of parliament on grounds of constitutional law. Still less would they advocate a reorganization of the representative system to satisfy popular or colonial desires. And yet they admitted the provocation of serious grievances at home and in America. Their only course was to attack the actual conduct of the existing ministry, and by so doing lay themselves open to the charge of factious opposition. . . .

Whig inactivity in American affairs between 1770 and 1774 appears at first sight to require some explanation, even though it was but part of a lull which pervaded the entire country. Whig fortunes were at a low ebb during this period. The break with Chatham had been followed by divisions and defections; and the miscellaneous elements, united only in opposition to the ministry, added to the appearance of a purely factious desire for places. The association of the whigs with the rights of property at home, in Ireland, and in the East India Company gave little opportunity for rallying wide support.

There was, moreover, a convergence of opinion on American affairs. The king and the whigs both sought to maintain the authority of parliament. Chatham wished to preserve it as a governing power without violating the constitutional safeguards of property against taxation. There was little practical difference between Chatham's insistence that parliament had no right to tax America and Burke's desire to preserve the right but to refrain from exercising it. Even within the ministry the hope of taxation was dwindling, and Franklin commented in 1771 that the doctrine was almost generally given up. All that remained was the dignity of parliament and the refusal to recede as far as a formal renunciation.

The Final Blow

The final blow to a whig program of resistance on American affairs came in 1772 with the appointment of Lord Dartmouth as secretary of state in charge of the colonial department. Dartmouth was a former member of the Rockingham ministry and had preserved a close connection with the group. His integrity was above suspicion, and his desire for conciliation well known. His acceptance of office was therefore a very different matter from the defection of Germain and Cornwall about the same time. It was rather the carrying of whig policies into the ministerial camp, the more since the intimacy of Dartmouth with North gave good reason for the belief that his conciliatory disposition was shared in higher quarters. With Dartmouth in the office principally concerned with America, instead of the harsh and authoritarian Hillsborough, the whigs could hardly launch a successful campaign against the ministry. . . .

When the Quebec Bill first came before parliament in May, 1774, it faced unqualified and unanimous opposition from whigs and radicals. Only the grounds of attack varied with different individuals. Some denounced the acceptance of the Roman Catholic faith as the religion of the colony; others attacked the appointive council, which replaced an elected assembly; others, the establishment of French civil law; and all, the extension of the area of the province to include the back country west of the English colonies. On the whole, the Rockingham whigs were the more moderate in their attacks. Burke carefully refrained from raising the religious issue, and he and his friends led a campaign directed chiefly against the constitutional provisions of the bill. The governmental provisions were in their view reactionary, and even indicated a "legal parliamentary despotism," fortified by the revenues of Quebec, at the uncontrolled disposal of the treasury. The mode of thought in these arguments is further shown by Burke's allusion to the people whom he regarded as affected by the bill. These were, in order, English

merchants, English subjects, and Canadians. While, therefore, the Rockingham whigs may have represented the more
conservative opposition, it is clear that they were thinking
primarily of English commercial and constitutional interests. By far the loudest argument was the cry of "despotism,"
the time-honored whig war cry; and Burke with all his moderation can hardly have appreciated the critical situation of
British power in Canada when he proposed a year's delay in
the consideration of the bill. The main grounds of opposition were constitutional, but the whigs were now thinking
also of the American point of view. In this respect, therefore,
the way was opening for America to be made the main rallying point of opposition.

Sam Adams's Role in Encouraging Revolution

John C. Miller

One of the most influential historians of the revolutionary era, John C. Miller focuses his attention on the pivotal individual Samuel Adams. Adams, a colonial rabble-rouser turned revolutionary, tried to incite the citizens of Boston to rise up against British soldiers occupying the city. In this selection, Miller focuses on the Boston Massacre and Sam Adams's role in both the events leading up to and the aftermath of the riot.

British troops had marched into Boston unopposed, but Sam Adams did not propose to allow them to enjoy long the hospitality of the Puritan metropolis. Rather than provide barracks for the soldiers, Adams was resolved to let them freeze in their encampment on the Boston Common. Whigs were told to show redcoats the same courtesy they did "Serpents and Panthers," and Sam Adams felt that even the Common in the dead of winter was too good for them. Adams insisted that, since the General Court had not consented to receive the troops, they had no right whatever to be in Massachusetts; and he construed the Mutiny Act, by which Parliament had provided the manner and place of billeting royal troops in the colonies, to rule them out of Boston and station them in Castle William, three miles out to sea. Boston selectmen and the Massachusetts Council supported Adams in refusing to quarter the soldiers in Boston, but the British military authorities were determined to post them in the heart of town until the citizens had been thoroughly cured of their weakness for rioting. If the regiments were put in Castle William,

Excerpted from John C. Miller, *Sam Adams: Pioneer in Propaganda* (Boston: Little, Brown, 1936). Copyright 1936 by John C. Miller. Reprinted by permission of the John C. and Gladys J. Miller Trust.

Boston Sons of Liberty might tar and feather Tories and Commissioners at will before order could be restored. Consequently, Boston warehouses were converted into barracks and the metropolis was garrisoned with redcoats whose "spirit-stirring drum and ear-piercing fife" grated discordantly with the "sweet songs, violins, and flutes, of the serenading Sons of Liberty" until the Boston Massacre.[1]

With four regiments of British regulars in Boston, many of the Sons of Liberty began to cover up their attempts to incite resistance with a less stiff-necked bearing toward the "invaders." After patriotically preventing the soldiers from being housed elsewhere in Boston, William Molineux tried to rent out for a garrison a warehouse on Wheelwright's wharf in which he had an interest; and James Otis sent General Gage his card and an invitation to dinner which the general firmly declined. Parliament almost threw these uneasy patriots into a panic by reviving a statute of Henry VIII to transport Americans suspected of treason to England for trial. Adams felt safe with a Boston jury which was certain to be loaded with Sons of Liberty, but he knew that English jurors would show him small mercy. Tories and Crown officers hopefully awaited the "Doom of Boston"; and Thomas Hutchinson began taking depositions to speed Adams and his crew on their way to Tyburn. Wagers were offered in Boston that Adams, Hancock, and Otis would swing from the gallows, and it was whispered among Tories that Adams "shuddered at the sight of hemp." In London, the King's friends remarked "with a snear" that James Otis, the mad Bostonian, would soon have an opportunity to "defend the assumed rights of the New World at the bar of the House of Commons."[2] But a rude disappointment was in store for the British Tories who promised themselves huge diversion from this cargo of transported American Whigs. The Mass-

1. *The Works of John Adams*, II, 213; X, 199. *The Writings of Samuel Adams*, I, 249–250; II, 48, 49, 392.   2. Andrew Oliver, *op. cit.*, Andrew Oliver to John Spooner, Oct. 28, 1768. *Chalmers Papers*, III, Sparks MSS., Harvard College Library; Thomas Hutchinson to Lord Hillsborough, April 27, 1770. *The Correspondence of Thomas Gage*, 1763–1775, edited by Clarence E. Carter (1933), II, 501. *Hess-Wendell Papers*, MSS. Mass. Hist. Soc., Edmund Quincy to John Wendell, Jan. 17, 1769. *Boston Gazette*, Jan. 23, 1769.

achusetts patriots had been too cautious to run their necks into a noose. No treason could be proved against them, although the attorney-general found that they had come "within an hair's breadth of it." By this slim margin, Otis and Adams were spared the Tower. The Whigs quickly recovered from their fright and, when they saw that the Ministry intended to pocket the affront, they became "more assuming and tyrannical than before."[3] After the Massachusetts Convention, bluffing was thought to be a besetting sin of Bostonians, but when the British government let the patriot leaders go scot-free after having threatened them with being drawn and quartered on Tyburn, it was clear that British Tories were as mighty blusterers as the Boston Whigs. By this unexpected change of policy, American patriots were encouraged to regard the menaces of the British government as empty gestures which would never be carried out. . . .

The Pot Begins to Boil

In the summer of 1769 the British government planned to withdraw two of the four regiments of British regulars from Boston—to the great consternation of many Crown officers, who feared that the remaining troops would be unable to hold the Sons of Liberty in check. Governor Bernard believed that what was really required was "a Reinforcement of the King's Forces at Boston [rather] than a weakening of them." When Sam Adams learned that it was proposed to reduce the Boston garrison he immediately presented a set of resolves to the House of Representatives so seditious that Commodore Hood declared they were "of a more extraordinary nature, than any that have yet passed an American Assembly." Just as the Sixty-fourth Regiment was about to embark for Halifax, Adams published these resolves—which, in effect, denied all Parliamentary authority over the colony— in the *Boston Gazette*, although they had not yet passed the House of Representatives. This "alarm bell to revolt" so frightened the Crown officers that the embarkation was sus-

3. *Debates in the House of Commons, Reports of Sir Henry Cavendish* (1841), I, 196. *Chalmers Papers*, III, Thomas Hutchinson to Lord Hillsborough, April 27, 1770.

pended and the troops were ordered back to their barracks lest the townspeople attempt to throw off British sovereignty and drive the remaining troops out of town. It was only after Adams's resolves had been repudiated by the House of Representatives that this alarm was allayed. When the town had quieted down, two regiments boarded the transports for Halifax, leaving less than five hundred effective regulars in Boston to keep order. The patriots were now more than a match for the troops and Hutchinson's misgivings deepened that there would soon be bloodshed in the metropolis.[4]

Early in the spring of 1770 the situation in Boston passed entirely out of control of the peace officers. Sam Adams's "Mohawks" brawled with redcoats in taverns and back alleys while the ropewalkers picked quarrels with the Twenty-ninth Regiment—those guardians of law and order whose bad tempers were the terror of sober citizens whether Whig or Tory. Then, in March 1770, an incident occurred which led directly to the Boston Massacre. Samuel Gray, one of the hardiest brawlers employed at Gray's ropewalk in Boston, asked a soldier of the Twenty-ninth Regiment if he wanted a job. When the man answered that he did, Gray said he had a privy that needed cleaning. This insult provoked an immediate fight between the soldiers and ropewalkers, but no serious clash took place until their pent-up animosity burst forth on March 5, 1770.

One morning shortly before that day, the citizens of Boston awoke to find the streets plastered with notices, signed by many of the soldiers garrisoned in the town, that the troops intended to attack the townspeople. This startling news threw the town into a ferment, for apparently few citizens doubted the genuineness of these papers. It is singular, nevertheless, that the soldiers should have given their plans away in this manner if they really contemplated an attack

4. *Bernard Papers*, VII, Bernard to Lord Hillsborough, July 7, 1769. Public Record Office, Admiralty Secretary, In Letters, 483, Lib. Cong., 25, Commodore Hood to Philip Stevens, July 10, 1769. Letters of Samuel Cooper to Pownall and Franklin, 1770-74, Bancroft Transcripts, New York Public Library, Samuel Cooper to Thomas Pownall, July 12, 1769. *Bernard Papers*, VII, Bernard to Lord Hillsborough, July 7, 1769. Hutchinson, III, 242.

and that they signed their names to documents that might be used as damning evidence against them. These notices were doubtless forgeries made by Adams and his followers and posted during the night by the "Loyall Nine" to produce an explosion that would sweep Boston clear of redcoats; for during the Massacre trials it is significant that the prosecution did not enter them as evidence of the soldiers' guilt. The events of the night of March 5 bear out this explanation of their origin. That evening a crowd of small boys began to snowball the British sentry in King's Street. Pelting the redcoats had become a recognized pastime among the Whigs, but it was soon apparent that this was to be no ordinary evening in Boston, for both soldiers and civilians had been convinced by Adams's propaganda that they were in danger of massacre from their enemies. After the sentry had sent his tormentors scampering, crowds of townspeople began to gather and head for King's Street. The square before the customhouse was soon filled with a swearing, turbulent mass of men, many of whom were armed with clubs, staves, and formidable pieces of jagged ice. Although Sam Adams and other patriots carefully avoided calling this crowd a mob, John Adams declared the name too good for it—a "motley rabble of saucy boys, negroes and mulattoes, Irish teagues and outlandish jack tars," he said, had turned out to fight the troops. Among them were Samuel Gray, the ropewalker who had started a free-for-all a few days before by inviting a soldier to clean his outhouse; Crispus Attucks, a huge mulatto noted for his prowess with the cudgel; James Caldwell, a ship's mate; and Patrick Carr, a seasoned Irish rioter. These stout cudgel-boys had beaten up so many redcoats that the sentry hastily summoned the main guard, which, led by Captain Preston of the Twenty-ninth Regiment, tumbled out eagerly for a fight. Consequently, the mob found itself face to face with its worst enemies; pellets of ice, sticks, and cudgels flew fast; and a large body of citizens who had gathered in Dock Square, where a mysterious gentleman in a red cloak and red wig harangued them to make a concerted attack upon the troops, rushed to join the brisk work that was going on before the customhouse. It was a wild scene even to Bostonians hardened to "Pope Day" riots and patriotic demonstrations; as John Adams later described it, "the multitude was shouting and huzzaing, and threatening life, the bells ringing, the mob whistling, screaming and rending like an Indian yell, the people from all quarters throwing every species of rubbish they could pick up in the streets."[5] Meanwhile, the ringing of bells all over Boston and the near-by towns was bringing hundreds of reënforcements to the mob in King's Street. Thus far, the soldiers had used their bayonets to keep the mob at bay and no patriot had suffered worse casualty than a smart rap on the shins. In spite of the hail of missiles, the soldiers withheld their fire until the mob screamed that the "bloody-backed rascals" did not dare to shoot. The troops restrained themselves with difficulty from giving Adams's "Mohawks" a taste of powder and ball, but when one of them was sent sprawling by a patriot brickbat he recovered his gun and fired directly into the mob. Most of the soldiers likewise opened fire,—at Captain Preston's order, many of the town's witnesses later testified,—and after they had emptied their guns five civilians had been killed or mortally wounded.

The "Victims" of the Massacre

The victims were typical members of the Boston mob: Samuel Gray, Crispus Attucks, James Caldwell, and Patrick Carr all fell in the British fire. Samuel Maverick, the fifth victim, was an apprentice who had taken no part in the riot. John Adams said that those killed in the Massacre were "the most obscure and inconsiderable that could have been found upon the continent," but Sam Adams made them pure and holy martyrs to liberty.[6] Crispus Attucks, the Framingham mulatto, a veteran of a score of riots, was exalted with the rest, although it was common knowledge that he had led an army of thirty sailors armed with clubs in Cornhill on the night of March 5 and that it was chiefly his violent assault upon the troops that had caused bloodshed. Only one of the

5. Frederick Kidder, *The Boston Massacre* (1870), 255–257.　6. *The Works of John Adams*, IX, 352.

victims, Patrick Carr, was denied the sweets of martyrdom by Sam Adams, because his deathbed confession absolved the soldiers of all blame for the Massacre.

Adams's Role in Publicizing the Massacre

Sam Adams lost no time in making the most of the "Bloody Work in King's Street." The day after the Massacre, the town meeting was called in Faneuil Hall, where Adams made such a rousing speech from the rostrum that his hearers declared it was "enough to fire any heart with a desire to become a patriot."[7] Having thrown the citizens into this bristling frame of mind, Adams demanded the immediate withdrawal of the British troops from Boston. This, the townspeople agreed, was the only way to prevent further "blood and carnage." Adams thereupon placed himself and Hancock at the head of a town committee and marched to the Town House overlooking the scene of the Massacre, where, in the Council chamber hung with the portraits of Charles II and James II and "little miserable likenesses" of the Puritan magistrates, Adams laid his demands before the Council. At the head of the Council table sat Lieutenant Governor Hutchinson; at his right, Colonel Dalrymple, commander in chief of His Majesty's forces in Boston; and around the table were seated twenty-eight councilors wearing "large white wigs, English scarlet cloth cloaks."[8] Standing before these dignitaries as spokesman for the citizens of Boston, Adams described the "dangerous, ruinous, and fatal effects of standing armies in populous cities in time of peace," the hatred of New Englanders toward the troops who had spilled patriot blood, and repeated the resolves of the Boston town meeting demanding the immediate removal of the soldiers from the metropolis. Hutchinson answered that since he had no authority over the King's troops nothing could be done until he had consulted the home government. But Adams was not to be put off so easily; he instantly appealed to the Massachusetts charter by which

7. *New York Journal or General Advertiser*, March 29, 1770. 8. *The Works of John Adams*, X, 250.

Hutchinson was constituted commander in chief of all the military and naval forces within the province. When Hutchinson and Dalrymple saw that Adams was determined to force their hand, they laid their heads together and, after

Actions of the Mob

Taken from a letter from a man in Boston, this excerpt describes the actions of a mob in August 1765. It is easy to see how a mob out of control could provoke a serious act of violence like the Boston Massacre.

In the Morning of the 27th Inst. between five and six a Mob Assembled and Erected a Gallows near the Town House and then Dispers'd, and about Ten A Clock Reassembled and took the Effigys of the Above Men and the Stamp Master and Carted them up Thames Street, then up King Street to the said Gallows where they was hung up by the Neck and Suspended near 15 feet in the Air, And on the Breast of the Stamp Master, was this Inscription THE STAMP MAN, and holding in his Right hand the Stamp Act, And upon the Breast of the Doct'r was wrote, THAT INFAMOUS, MISCREATED, LEERING JACOBITE DOCT'R MURFY. In his Right hand was a folded Letter with this Direction To that Mawgazeene of Knowledge Doct'r Muffy in Rhode Island, And on the Same Arm was Wrote, If I had but Rec'd this Letter from the Earl of Bute But One Week sooner. And upon a strip of paper hanging out of his Mouth was wrote It is too late Martinius to Retract, for we are all Aground.

And upon Mr. Howard's Breast was wrote, THAT FAWNING, INSIDIOUS, INFAMOUS MISCREANT AND PARACIDE MARTINIUS SCRIBLERIUS, and upon his Right Arm was wrote, THE ONLY FILIAL PEN. Upon his left Arm was wrote, CURS'D AMBITION AND YOUR CURSED CLAN HAS RUIN'D ME and upon the Same Arm a little Below was this, WHAT THO' I BOAST OF INDEPENDENCE POSTERITY WILL CURSE MY MEMORY. And upon one of the Posts of the Gallows was wrote, We have an Hereditary Indefeasible Right to a Halter, Besides we Encourag'd the Growth of Hemp you know. And Underneath that, was a New Song (made upon the Occasion) which I have here Inclos'd. And upon the other

much whispering, offered to remove the Twenty-ninth Regiment, which alone had fired upon the citizens, to Castle William and to keep the other regiment confined to quarters in Boston. But here again Hutchinson played into Adams's

Post was wrote That Person who shall Efface this Publick Mark of Resentment will be Deem'd an Enemy to liberty and Accordingly meet with Proper Chastisement. And about five A Clock in the Afternoon they made a Fire under the Gallows which Consum'd the Effigy's, Gallows and all, to Ashes. I forgot to tell you that a Boot hung over the Doctor's Shoulder with the Devil Peeping out of it etc. I've Inclos'd you a piece that was Stuck up in the Town House at the Same time. And after the Effigys were Burnt the Mob Dispers'd and we thought it was all Over. But last Night about Dusk they all Muster'd again, and first they went to Martin Howard's, and Broke Every Window in his house Frames and all, likewise Chairs Tables, Pictures and every thing they cou'd come across. they also Saw'd down two Trees which Stood before his door and Bro't them and Stuck them up in two Great Guns which have been fix"d at the Bottom of the Parade some Years as Posts. when they found they had Entirely Demolish'd all his Furniture and done what damage they Cou'd, They left his house, and Proceeded to Doctor Moffatts where they Behav'd much in the Same Manner. I Can't say which Came off the Worst, For all the Furniture of Both Houses were Entirely Destroy'd, Petitions of the houses broke down, Fences Level'd with the Ground and all the Liquors which were in Both Houses were Entirely Lost. Dear Doctor this Moment I've Rec'd a Peace of News with Effects me so Much that I Cant write any More, which is the Demolition of your worthy Daddy's house and Furniture etc. But I must Just let you know that the Stamp Master has Resign'd, the Copy of His Resignation and Oath I now Send you. I hope, my Friend You'll Send me the Particulars of your daddy's Misfortune. Yours for Ever

Stanley I. Kutler. *Looking for America: The People's History*. Vol. 1. New York: W.W. Norton, 1979.

hands. "In his venerable grey locks, and with his hands trembling under a nervous complaint," Adams told Hutchinson and Dalrymple that if they had "authority to remove one regiment they had authority to remove two," and that nothing short of a complete evacuation of the town by all the troops would preserve the peace of the province.[9] Unless the metropolis were cleared of redcoats, Adams warned, there would be more bloody work in Boston—this time with the King's troops as the victims. Fifteen thousand fighting men, he exclaimed, were ready to pour into Boston to take revenge upon the soldiers. Dalrymple needed little persuasion: he was well aware that he could not defend his position against the New England militia with the four hundred men he could bring into the field; and he had no desire to risk a disgraceful rout at the hands of farmers and Boston Sons of Liberty. When Adams made these threats he believed he saw Hutchinson's legs tremble and his face grow pale—"and," added Adams, "I enjoyed the Sight." For a few hours, Hutchinson planned to resist the townspeople, but when he saw "how artfully it was steered" by Adams, whose strategy had placed the entire responsibility of keeping the troops in Boston upon his shoulders, he acknowledged that he must either yield or leave the province. The Council assured Hutchinson that new England would soon be in arms against the troops and that "the night which was coming on would be the most terrible that was ever seen in America." The danger of defying the people was too great; before nightfall, Hutchinson struck his colors and Bostonians were promised the speedy removal of both regiments.[10] . . .

Adams's first thought was to convince the world that Boston was innocent of any blame for the Massacre. There was need of quick action, because immediately after the bloodshed, Robinson, the Commissioner of the Customs,

<hr/>

9. *Ibid.*, X, 252.   10. But the troops were not immediately removed from Boston. The delay greatly alarmed the Whigs, who continued to threaten Hutchinson and other Crown officers with an attack upon the troops. When the soldiers finally marched out of their barracks to the wharf from which they took ship to Castle William, it was necessary for William Molineux to march beside them to protect them from the hooting citizens. *The Works of John Adams*, X, 252, 253.

who had been most active in counterworking the Whigs, secretly left Boston for England with papers which the patriots suspected were to be used to prove Boston's guilt. To offset this Tory propaganda, Adams had himself, Hancock, and the Boston selectmen appointed a committee by the citizens to take *ex parte* testimony from witnesses and draw up an account of the Massacre for public consumption. Adams and his followers fell to work with such enthusiasm that they were soon attempting to prove that the Commissioners of the Customs had fired upon the citizens the night of the massacre and were as guilty as the soldiers of murdering unarmed Whigs. The patriots were eager to pin some fresh atrocity upon the Commissioners to render them more hateful to the people: therefore Adams proclaimed that he had ferreted out a conspiracy between the military officers and Commissioners of the Customs to slaughter Bostonians. "Some of the Banditti," remarked a Tory, referring to Adams and his fellow committeemen, "prevailed on a little French Boy belonging to Mainwaring [a customhouse officer] to swear he actually fired three Guns from the Custom House window under his Master's Directions." Moreover, Adams's examination of the witnesses seemed to prove conclusively that the soldiers and Commissioners were the sole aggressors and that the townspeople had been treated with "unexampled Barbarity"; but Tories said that Adams was forced to stoop to perjury and falsehood to save Boston's reputation. Had Hutchinson possessed authority to enforce his orders, he would have stopped Adams and the selectmen from taking testimony because he believed they were attempting to fasten the witnesses to signed affidavits before the trial took place—a procedure which would put the soldier's defense under a serious disadvantage. But before Hutchinson could act, the damage was done: the evidence was turned over to Adams and Bowdoin to be put into literary form. Robinson was already on his way to England, but Boston chartered a speedy vessel to carry its "Narrative" to the mother country; and although Robinson won the race, the patriots were not far behind with a cargo of red-hot propaganda with which to avert punishment by the British government.

The Trial of the Soldiers

Sam Adams was keenly aware of the necessity of bringing the soldiers to trial while the memory of the Massacre was still fresh. He bent every effort therefore to secure an early trial; and when it was reported that the illness of two judges would force a postponement until June, he headed a town committee to demand that Hutchinson appoint special judges immediately. At court, Adams made a "very *pathetic* Speech" in which he used such strong language that the Tories perceived that "the plain design of this Speech was, that gentlemen, you must comply with our demand."[11] The spectacle of Massachusetts royal judges "overawed and insulted" by such a raw plebeian as Sam Adams spurred Hutchinson to action. The governor knew that by opposing Adams he was risking another explosion in Boston: popular hostility toward the troops still blazed so fiercely that the patriot leaders themselves had difficulty in preventing another mob attack upon the soldiers before their final removal to Castle William, and there was constant danger that Preston would be dragged from prison for a lynching party at Liberty Tree.[12] Nevertheless, Hutchinson encouraged the judges to resist the patriots and, as a consequence, the trials were delayed until October 1770, over six months after the Massacre. Yet, even with this respite, it seemed unlikely that anything short of a royal pardon would save Preston and his men from a gibbet on the Boston Common.[13]

Despite Adams's eagerness to see the soldiers declared guilty, he urged John Adams and Josiah Quincy, two of the best lawyers in the patriot party, to undertake their defense. Preston's friends advised him to "stick at no reasonable fee" to secure the services of lawyers friendly to the Whig leaders, but it was Sam Adams's persuasion and John Adams's high sense of duty rather than the prospect of a fat fee that brought Josiah Quincy and John Adams to Preston's aid. Since 1768, when John Adams had yielded to Sam's impor-

---

11. *Chalmers Papers*, III, Narrative of Events in Boston. Peter Oliver, 123. *Boston Gazette*, March 19, 1770.   12. *The Works of John Adams*, X, 252, 253. Mass. Archives, 26, *Hutchinson Corr.*, II, 497, 525.   13. Thomas Gage to Thomas Hutchinson, April 30, 1770, MS. Mass. Hist. Soc.

tunities and entered Boston politics, he had risen high in the patriot party. His law partner, Josiah Quincy, was a promising young patriot who many Whigs believed would eventually step into James Otis's place at the head of the Massachusetts Country Party. It is singular that Sam Adams, who was never known to give his enemies an advantage, should have bestowed this array of legal talent upon men he hoped to convict of murder. Certainly, Adams had lost none of his rancor toward the "bloody-backed rascals" who had shed patriot blood in King's Street, nor had he failed to perceive that an acquittal would be a disastrous blow to the Boston Whigs. Adams's action sprang from his conviction that if patriot lawyers defended Preston and his men, the town's witnesses would not be cross-examined so closely as to bring to light evidence which proved Bostonians responsible for the Massacre. In John Adams, Sam did not mistake his man.

The younger Adams saw as clearly as did his cousin that Boston's reputation was at stake and that the town's witnesses should not be pressed too warmly: when Josiah Quincy's ardor for his clients caused him to interrogate sharply the prosecution's witnesses, John Adams quickly stopped him by declaring that unless Quincy ceased he would resign as counsel. Although John Adams encountered a "torrent of unpopularity" from the rank and file of the patriot party for defending the soldiers, it is significant that Sam Adams, far from bearing him resentment, praised him in the Boston newspapers for his conduct during the trial.[14]. . .

The Necessity of Fighting

Sam Adams used the Boston Massacre not only to embitter Americans toward Great Britain but to prove the necessity of fighting British troops before they had opportunity to gain a foothold in the country. The Massacre seemed to bear out Adams's contention that the King's soldiers should have been resisted when they reached Boston. It was futile, he preached in 1770, to look to the courts for redress; the militia, not judges and juries, must save new Englanders from military despotism. After the Massacre, Adams was joined by

14. Gordon, I, 291. *Boston Gazette*, Jan. 7, 1771, Harbottle Dorr Files, Mass. Hist. Soc.

a host of amateur generals who proposed to save New England by bringing the militia to full fighting strength and replacing the "ancient methods of bushing fighting" with modern strategy and formations. The seat of danger was no longer the frontier and redskins but the seaboard and redcoats; military tactics which were effective against Indians would be useless against British regulars—therefore, new Englanders must henceforth practise manœuvres in open fields and train themselves to meet large bodies of troops fighting in European fashion. The fiction of an impending French war that had proved so useful during the Massachusetts Convention was again employed to screen these preparations to wage war against British troops; and Sam Adams and his followers still talked of grappling with France while they prepared to fight England.[15]

Like other Whig leaders after the Boston Massacre, Sam Adams painted war as glorious and fostered those "generous and manly Sentiments, which usually attend a true Military Spirit." He was overjoyed to see how eagerly new Englanders cleaned their muskets and drilled in militia companies to prepare for the day when they should be compelled to fight for their liberties. Boston led the movement to build up a militia capable of holding its own against British regulars, and plans were laid to give the next army of British "invaders" a warm reception. When it was rumored that troops would be sent from England to punish Boston for attacking British soldiers on the night of the Massacre, the Sons of Liberty held a meeting in William Molineux's house to decide whether to oppose their landing; and Hutchinson did not doubt that if the force sent out from England were small, the patriots would fight. To set an example for New Englanders, Bostonians went through their military exercises every evening on the Common and declared openly that no royal troops would ever again land in the metropolis. "Innocence is no longer safe," exclaimed Adams and his followers, "we are now obliged to appeal to GOD and to our ARMS for defense."[16]

15. *Boston Evening Post*, April 30, 1770; June 11, 1770. *Boston Gazette*, Jan. 27, 1771; Feb. 24, 1772. *The Writings of Samuel Adams*, II, 68, 69.   16. *Boston Gazette*, April 12, 1770.

Chapter 2

The Faces of the Revolution: The People Who Fought the War and the Man Who Led Them

Turning|Points
IN WORLD HISTORY

The Revolutionaries of America

James Kirby Martin

Rutgers University historian James Kirby Martin compares and contrasts the types of revolutionaries that brought about the American Revolution. Martin, who also wrote *Men in Rebellion: Higher Governmental Leaders and the Coming of the American Revolution*, accurately shows the variations between the radical revolutionaries and the reluctant ones.

The most extreme form of human resistance, organized warfare in full-scale rebellion, set the erratic course in motion that led to Yorktown and the final severing of political ties with the British Empire. Yorktown was the beginning of the military end, but it by no means guaranteed the success of the American cause. Even before the war had reached its crescendo in the late summer and fall of 1776, erstwhile provincials were debating questions central to the future character and organization of American social and political institutions. No more important question was being asked than how "revolutionary" the rebellion should be permitted to become. Should there be a real revolution, a movement that was more than a mere uprising against the constituted authority of the King in Parliament? It would take years to formulate the answer.

The term revolution implied, then as now, profound alterations in economic, social, and political relationships. Although it did not necessarily denote a total rejection of past traditions and habits, it did suggest the creation of something new, uplifting, and beneficial for humanity. The most vexing and challenging question confronting rebellious Americans was how much change should be permitted. On that point there was wide disagreement.

While the war raged in the foreground, an awesome, if not potentially destructive, gap opened among those who were deciding how far the Revolution should proceed in reordering human relationships, that is, whether there should be more than a mere transfer of power and authority from the ruling elite in Britain to one in America. In the end, that bitter internal controversy caused as much confusion and instability in the republic as did the war itself or the problems of international diplomacy. War-related problems dominated at first after 1776, because everyone knew that all other questions were academic unless the military struggle resulted in favorable peace terms. But always alongside pressing military and diplomatic questions of the day stood the most disruptive issue of all—that of the potential form and character of the nascent republic. . . .

The Real Revolution

The rebellion had been successful in its military and diplomatic phases, yet the kinds of internal institutions and socioeconomic and political values and practices that would pervade the new nation were very much in the process of being determined. That process, involving the potential for real revolution, still threatened to tear apart from within what had triumphed from without.

The act of full-scale rebellion meant that the former colonists had to decide for themselves whether they would alter significantly political and social relationships. Thomas Jefferson made the issue paramount in the Declaration of Independence. In writing about "self-evident truths," and in envisioning governmental institutions that would protect and defend each citizen's right to life, liberty, and happiness, the Virginian had asked, circumspectly, about how revolutionary the American Revolution was to be. Earlier in 1776 John Adams had touched upon the same issue somewhat differently in discussing the nature of republics. He stressed that republican governments in past ages had been of "an inexhaustible variety, because possible combinations of the powers of society are capable of innumerable variations."

But all republican governments had common characteristics. They based their authority in the people and drew sovereign life from them. In principle, Adams explained, "the very definition of a republic is 'an empire of laws and not of men'." Representative governments, above all else, reflected and served popular needs; and they were wise and just in legislating for the best interests of all citizens.

Americans in 1776 were thus setting themselves apart from Britain's "corrupted" practices. The call for republicanism and the rule of law was a logical extension of perceptions about a conspiracy from above in the form of political tyranny. It was also the beginning of a definition of what the Revolution should seek to create—an experiment in republicanism in which all fit persons had access to authority; in which no one would be favored for the artificial reasons of family bloodline, social standing, personal wealth, or formal education; and in which all citizens who behaved virtuously and acted meritoriously in service to the community would have the actual responsibility for governing their peers through representative institutions. As the rebellion turned to full-scale warfare, then, it was necessary to institutionalize in reality what was at that moment a group of half-tested and half-tried political theories. For some insurgents, the assignment carried with it a larger mission as the redeemers and defenders of human liberty in a darkened world in which tyranny had all but snuffed out liberty and the light of human reason.

To make words come alive and have meaning in practice would not be easy for the former colonists. Theirs was a world that was becoming less rather than more equalitarian in the distribution of wealth and property. Theirs was a society in which the fashionable were becoming ever more imitative of English life-styles. Theirs was a society in which a burgeoning native elite was putting greater stress upon a formal hierarchy of privileges and distinctions according to artificial measures, a society in which the concept of deference still held exalted meaning. And it was a society in which black slaves, all women, indentured servants, and the propertyless poor—as much as 80 percent of the adult population—had neither *de jure* nor *de facto* political or social rights. In 1776 a citizen had to be a white adult male, with at least modest property holdings, to be eligible even to vote. It was a narrow base, although not necessarily narrow for its time. An important question was whether the base could or would be broadened by a generation dedicated to the institutionalization of human liberty.

It may have been gratifying to the insurgent leaders to speak of republicanism, sovereignty of the people, and the rule of law. But very few of these leaders were fully prepared to accept all of the implications of their words—and very few were willing to apply them to slaves, women, or indentured servants. Even those who considered the implications seriously thought primarily in political rather than in social terms. What the most radical among them sought were structures of government that excluded the possibility of monarchy and placed decision-making authority as close as possible to the people.

Indeed, what the small number of *radical* Revolutionary insurgents of 1776 had in common was an unbounded abstract faith in the people. In their personal social origins, many of these men were quite common; others had worked very closely with the colonial citizenry as popular leaders during the years of protest and resistance. Thomas Paine had not been a popular leader, but the commitment to sweeping change had been strongly evidenced in his writings. In *Common Sense* he stressed that the people were inherently *virtuous* and imbued with a capacity for self-sacrifice when it came to serving the greater good of the republican community. Monarchs had been the real source of bad behavior, the true corruptors: "It is easy to see that when Republican virtue fails, slavery ensues. Why is the constitution of England sickly, but because monarchy hath poisoned the Republic, the Crown hath engrossed the Commons?" Declare independence, leave behind the tainted monarchical past, Paine vehemently urged, and watch the people glorify the new nation by virtuously ruling themselves.

The transplanted British staymaker bluntly urged his readers to renounce their British political heritage (many

Americans believed that the English government had inherent republican qualities because the monarch was not all-powerful) and to cast aside notions about balanced government. Monarchy in the personage of the king or queen, and aristocracy in the form of the House of Lords, were nothing more than "the base remains of two ancient tyrannies, compounded with new Republican materials . . . in the persons of the Commons, on whose virtue depends the freedom of England." Seize upon these materials, Paine insisted, and create simple governments without constraining structural checks upon the popular will. Form governments close to and in the hands of the people and their elected representatives. Have annually elected state assemblies, with only a national congress above these popularly based bodies charged with bringing the states together in realizing the nation's republican strength. Emphasize structural simplicity and popular sovereignty; place full trust in the virtuous citizenry. Paine's was clearly a radical vision in 1776.

Inherent in Paine's program was the idea of the regeneration of mankind through the model of a republican government. It would wean citizens from the lure of offices, titles, honors, power, and property accumulation as ends unto themselves and lead them toward what Jefferson, five months later would describe as the pursuit of happiness. . . .

Reluctant Revolutionaries

In juxtaposition to the radical Revolutionaries of 1776 were those leaders who may be classified as *reluctant* Revolutionaries. For purposes of comparative analysis, it seems appropriate to conceptualize differences in thoughts and attitudes among radical and reluctant Revolutionaries along a continuum of possibilities starting at one end with those who fully trusted in the people's virtue. At the other end were those who did not in any way trust the people and who believed that the democracy of citizens was as fully capable of abusing power and despoiling liberty as were willful monarchs. Reluctant Revolutionaries were generally more attached to traditional forms and practices; they had faith in institutions which balanced societal interests and social orders and encouraged orderliness and deference from the "common herd," as they continually thought of the people well after 1776. They viewed structural restraints as vital for protecting men of property and high standing from popular convulsions from below. They often characterized the latter by the phrase "democratic licentiousness"—the obverse of public virtue in government and society. One New Yorker summarized these attitudes as well as anyone: "No one loves Liberty more than I do, but of all Tyranny I most dread that of the Multitude."

Wedded in varying degrees to the conception of hierarchical and balanced government, the reluctant Revolutionaries of 1776 found themselves suspended in time and space between the British monarchy and its corrupting minions above them and the American people below them. Unlike their loyalist counterparts, with whom they shared many attitudes, the reluctant Revolutionaries could envision an American society surviving the transfer of power from a corrupted Britain to an uncorrupted America. Moreover, they could countenance concepts of republicanism and the rule of law. Yet like their loyalist counterparts, they could not approve of vesting power fully in the people. That conjured up to them visions of social and political chaos and doom.

Thus the reluctant Revolutionaries, a number of whom had been reconciliationists in the second Continental Congress, insisted that new American governments of the balanced variety had to be well established before the independence movement deteriorated into a state of anarchy. While some acts of anti-imperial violence had been condoned by them as necessary for checking tyranny, the reluctant Revolutionaries fretted incessantly about popular disturbances that had not been anti-imperial but rather had been directed against men like themselves—of property and of cautiously Whiggish persuasion. For instance, there had been the Paxton Boy uprising in central Pennsylvania during 1763, when Scots-Irish frontiersmen had got out of hand by killing innocent Indians in mindless retaliation for tribal depredations associated with Pontiac's Rebellion. Then, in early 1764, the boys marched toward Philadelphia with sinister threats about attacking the city unless the provincial government did something for the protection of western settlers. . . .

Advocating independence and favoring significant Revolutionary change simply did not follow parallel lines. Almost all reconciliationists were reluctant Revolutionaries. But radical Revolutionaries who were not intense independence advocates did not exist. And there were quite a number of independence men who were reluctant Revolutionaries. The primary issue was how much the people could be trusted in a republican polity with *de facto* power. Thomas Paine had no doubts, but there were many others who felt that they had compelling evidence that tyranny and the destruction of liberties could come as easily from below as from above. . . .

State Constitutions

Between 1774 and the end of 1777, ten of the thirteen rebellious American colonies—Massachusetts, Rhode Island, and Connecticut were the exceptions—adopted new constitutions. The Massachusetts insurgents, facing a fully developed military conflict in 1775, kept their charter of 1691 as the foundation of government, while dropping all trappings of British authority. In 1780 the citizenry adopted, although by a slim margin, a new constitution stressing balanced relationships. Rhode Island and Connecticut retained their liberal seventeenth-century charters—even governors and councilors had been popularly elected—while deleting all references to British sovereignty. Everywhere else insurgent leaders, meeting at first in extralegal congresses and conventions, eventually drafted constitutions, as the Virginians were doing in the spring of 1776. The provisions of the new state constitutions in turn became one expression of the extent of Revolutionary sentiment. They represented universally a commitment to the abstract principle of popular sovereignty, but, structurally, a weaker commitment to full-blown popular rule.

The state constitutions, in fact, exhibited the vast range of possibilities which can be distributed along the continuum suggested by the differences separating Thomas Paine (democratic republicanism) and Carter Braxton (republicanism by stewardship of the talented, the proved, and the wise).

Pennsylvania came closest to writing Paine's democratic sentiments into basic law. Its constitution of 1776 provided for an all-powerful, annually elected unicameral assembly. Pennsylvanians thus gained the right to govern themselves without traditional upper-hierarchy structural checks, except that there was an elected executive council which provided for the daily administration of government—it had no legislative functions. To ensure that decision making was as open as possible, citizens were given the right to attend legislative sessions; also proposed legislation had to be published in the newspapers before the final vote by the assembly. The constitution also provided for a council of censors to meet once every seven years for a full-range review of legislation. The censors had the authority to declare null and void any piece of legislation inconsistent with the constitution. All adult males could vote, provided they had resided in the state for at least a year; representation was to be according to the geographic distribution of population; and no representative could hold an assembly seat for more than four years out of seven. This precluded the possibility, according to the "rotation-in-office" principle, of "the danger of establishing an inconvenient [elected] aristocracy" with the ability to abuse power and flout the popular will endlessly through manipulation of the enfranchised at election time. If one believed in balanced government, the Pennsylvania constitution was radical. And reluctant Revolutionaries in and out of the state disliked it intensely.

The constitution of neighboring Maryland represented the other end of the continuum. Not only did reluctant Revolutionaries there retain the three traditional branches, but they also adopted ascending levels of property requirements for officeholding in each. Delegates to the lower house had to own at least a fifty-acre freehold; senators had to possess real and personal property worth a minimum of £1,000 current money; and the governor had to hold a minimum of £5,000 in real and personal property, £1,000 of which was to be in a freehold estate. To vote for delegates, white male citizens had to own property valued at a minimum of £30 current money, less than had been the case in the old regime.

The constitution provided that these same freeholders also were to name senatorial electors (men with at least £500 in property), who in turn were to meet separately and elect the upper house. The governor was to be elected by a joint ballot of the lower and upper houses. While the governor and delegates to the lower house served annual terms, senators were to hold office for five years. As men of more than modest property holdings, they were to be the stabilizing influence against popular excesses. Moreover, only the governor was limited in tenure by the rotation-in-office rule (he was able to serve only three in every seven years consecutively). The constitution also constrained the full range of prerogatives which governors under the Baltimore family had enjoyed, such as extensive patronage privileges and the power to adjourn assemblies and veto legislation. . . .

The other state constitutions generally fell on the continuum somewhere between Maryland's elitist and Pennsylvania's democratic models. New Hampshire, North Carolina, and Georgia came closest to Pennsylvania, demonstrating the least concern for balance and stewardship,while New York, Virginia, and South Carolina shared more in common with Maryland. New Jersey and Delaware were somewhere in the middle. Important general trends included a sharp reduction in gubernatorial powers and the lodging of extensive decision-making authority in the lower houses of assemblies. In a few cases, the executive branch ceased to exist or only had ceremonial functions. There was a general lowering of property requirements for voting as well as for holding statewide offices, and many more positions than ever before became directly or indirectly elective. Many constitutions specifically prohibited the kind of plural officeholding that some prerevolutionary Crown appointees had fed upon. Certainly these trends represented significant gains for the people, especially in the sense that no constitution rejected the principle of popular sovereignty. As embodied in the state constitutions, the first Revolutionary settlement was surprisingly enlightened for its time, though certainly tempered in some states by the restraining influence of the reluctant Revolutionaries.

The sum and substance of the written state constitutions, however, did not represent a linear victory for the Revolutionary citizenry. Property qualifications did not cease to exist, nor did all offices become directly elective. The old notion that citizens should have a propertied stake in society before they could participate in political matters did not die out; nor did the concepts of hierarchy, deference, and stewardship. All told, the constitutions may be viewed as going further toward popular rule than the reluctant Revolutionaries would have liked but certainly not as far (except perhaps for Pennsylvania) as the radical Revolutionaries would have preferred. Whatever the structural arrangements, community elite leaders rushed into the void created by the downfall of British leadership. The Patrick Henrys replaced the Lord Dunmores everywhere. Frustrated insurgent leaders maximized their political aspirations in the process—and they were doing so in support of liberty and the people.

Whether or not the process of state constitution making in the Revolutionary settlement of 1776 represented a democratizing trend was less important in shaping the future course of events than contemporary individual perceptions about that process. Thomas Jefferson believed that it was a satisfactory settlement: "The people seemed to have deposited the monarchical and taken up the republican government with as much ease as would have attended their throwing off an old and putting on a new suit of clothes. . . . A half dozen aristocratical gentlemen agonizing under the loss of preeminence have sometime ventured their sarcasms on our political metamorphosis. They have been thought fitter objects for pity than punishment." Another Virginian, who took "a view of our new Assembly, now sitting—under the happy auspices of the People only," declared excitedly that "though it is composed of men not quite so well dressed, nor so politely educated, nor so highly born as some Assemblies I have formerly seen—yet upon the whole I like their Proceedings—and upon the whole rather better than formerly." What endeared the spectacle to him was that the assembly now consisted of "the People's men (and the People in general are right.)" The new delegates were more "plain and of consequence less disguised, but I believe to be full[y] as honest, less intriguing, more sincere.". . .

Appearances of a radical break with prerevolutionary leadership traditions were thus as deceptive as they were real. But that did not matter to the reluctant Revolutionaries. They did not count, measure, and quantify before they formed their conclusions. As one of them stated: "A pure democracy may possibly do, when patriotism is the ruling passion but when the state abounds in rascals, as is the case with too many this day, you must suppress a little of that popular spirit." Many reluctant Revolutionaries simply never accepted the first Revolutionary settlement. Rather, they shared their dire predictions of impending doom with one another and looked for opportunities after 1776 to readjust it.

The British Opposition Press Supported the American Cause

Solomon Lutnick

Edmund Burke and the British Opposition press gave support to the American colonists as they pursued equal
rights under British law. Solomon Lutnick is a professor
of history who has researched the role of the press during
the American Revolution. Lutnick's description of the
battle between Britain's government-controlled papers
and the Opposition reveals that Britain's loyalties were divided over the issue of Americans' rights at the outset of
the American Revolution.

Looking back over the blunders that allowed a civil war
eventually to grow into a world conflict in which almost all
Europe was arrayed against Britain, John Fielding's *Courant*,
on August 11, 1781, denounced those few remaining Englishmen who were still "so destitute of principle" as to claim
the "virtue" of political impartiality. "In this hour of ministerial turpitude," it asserted, "every honest man cries out
shame upon . . . those creatures and those prints, that affect
an impartiality." Most newspapers, however, deviated from
their pledges of impartiality, and the war in America was reported by a London press hostile to the North ministry long
before news of Lexington and Concord forced Englishmen
to choose sides in their civil war. . . .

Unfortunately for London's Opposition press, the Marquis
of Rockingham, the most powerful leader of the Opposition,
thought almost as little of public opinion as did his monarch.
Although the radical London press demanded a change in the
Ministry and Rockingham stood to profit most from this

Reprinted from *The American Revolution and the British Press, 1775–1783*, by
Solomon Lutnick, by permission of the University of Missouri Press. Copyright
©1967 by the Curators of the University of Missouri.

change, there was no direct connection between the Marquis and the London editors. As long as Rockingham saw no need to alter the system of parliamentary representation that the city radicals thundered so heavily against, there could be little political rapport between the ostensible head of the Opposition in Parliament and the Opposition press. . . .

Edmund Burke wrote regularly for James Dodsley's *Annual Register*, and his large and talented family also helped place puffs and longer articles favorable to him in the newspapers. On March 13, 1779, appeared the first issue of a short-lived Opposition publication, *The Englishman*. Sponsored by Richard Brinsley Sheridan and apparently financed by the Duchess of Devonshire, this twice-weekly newspaper came to include some of the finest satirical essays of the era. Sheridan signed his own contributions "D," while Fox's essay in the March 14 edition was signed "Z." Richard Tickell, who was Sheridan's brother-in-law, and Richard Burke also were major contributors. On June 2, however, the final issue of the entertaining but unprofitable *Englishman* was published. Sheridan was now busily penning *The Critic*, and in late 1780 he would enter Parliament from Stafford. Thanks again to the Duchess of Devonshire, he would keep his seat for twenty-six years, while becoming not only one of England's outstanding playwrights, but after 1783 one of its most important newspaper managers. So, while Rockingham remained uncommunicative, three of his most ardent supporters saw to it that at least a semblance of a united Opposition appeared in the press.

In an attempt to counter these measures and bring public opinion over to its side, the Ministry not only badgered Opposition publications, but it also hired writers and paid publishers in order to place its point of view in many of the leading journals. The idea of hiring writers or even of purchasing a complete newspaper operation for the purpose of establishing a Government "house organ" was not new to eighteenth-century Englishmen. Robert Walpole, while First Minister, had made an art of manipulating public opinion (in 1742 the Committee of Secrecy discovered that over £50,000 of Secret Service funds had been paid to pamphleteers and to Treasury newspapers in the last decade of his administration), and Professor Namier has demonstrated that Newcastle, in the reign of George II, paid £4,000 to the hired journalists and pamphleteers who comprised his "propaganda department." By 1774 John Almon had charged that the Ministry was repeating its technique of a decade earlier (the Administration of the Earl of Bute) in order to deceive the nation by hiring writers and newspapers and by printing immense numbers of pamphlets that were sent through the mails, free of postage and expense, to every part of the kingdom. Almon accused, among others, the hired pens of Samuel Johnson, James Macpherson, William Knox, and Israel Mauduit of "deluding and duping" the nation as to the true state of affairs in America. At the same time, Thomas Townshend attacked Lord North in the Commons because of the pensions bestowed by the King "On those notorious Jacobites" Samuel Johnson and John Shebbeare. On October 3, 1775, "DETECTOR" made it clear in the *Morning Post* that liberty of the press, one of England's "greatest blessings and dearest privileges," was in jeopardy because "needy and profligate writers," hired by the Administration, were subverting this liberty by writing "with a pensioned hand" rather than with honest and honorable political motives. "DETECTOR" also gave the alerted reader some of the pen names used by the most prominent "ministerial scribblers." Five years later "BRITANNICUS," writing in the *Public Advertiser,* made the same charges. Both of these anonymous authors did not know, but would not have been surprised to learn, that John Robinson, North's Secretary to the Treasury, was indeed paying printers and authors for the publication of anti-American tracts. . . .

Bias in the British Press

The story of the war in America could not be told impartially. Because the Government could—and did—at pleasure withhold some official accounts and distort others, its versions of the news were regularly attacked by the Opposition press, which maintained that its own sources either entirely contradicted the official versions of the news reported in the *London Gazette* or else illuminated some glaring, and usually embarrassing, governmental omissions. The Secretaries of State were responsible for the publication of the *London Gazette*, and any profits that accrued from its sales were deemed perquisites of office and were duly shared between them. It was the task of the American Department to select the news and dispatches from the Colonies that were to be published. From the day in 1770 when he was appointed as Under Secretary of State for America in 1782, when the Shelburne ministry abolished the position, William Knox chose the official items of war news Englishmen were permitted to read. Knox knew more about America than did most of his contemporaries in the Government. From 1757 to 1761 he had been Provost Marshal of Georgia. For the next four years he was the London agent for Georgia and East Florida; he was removed from that position by the Colonies for writing a pamphlet defending the Stamp Act. While Knox's reputation as a propagandist was enhanced in 1775 with the publication of *The Claim of the Colonies to Exemption from Taxes imposed by Authority of Parliament, examined*, he rarely published anything subsequently. There is no evidence that Knox ever wrote to or for any newspapers or magazines while serving in the American Department, but the extreme confidence placed in him by his superior, Lord George Germain, rendered Knox vulnerable to the Opposition, which was certain that he was regularly writing to the press in defense of the Ministry and its American policies.

Knox and the *London Gazette* made certain that good news from the Colonies traveled fast, but, as one editor asserted, when bad news was to be disseminated, "it was some days before the accounts are sufficiently garbled, to be laid before the public; and it is generally some weeks before half the truth is really known." As soon as rumor of an important action in America spread, readers waited for the next edition of the tri-weekly *Gazette* or for a *Gazette Extraordinary*, and if no clarifying information appeared in the royal publication, they assumed that "the news was of such a nature as the Ministry thought improper to be published." The Opposition press regularly advised its readers to distrust the "nonsense and falsehoods" of the *London Gazette*. The *Westminster Journal* called the *Gazette's* compilers "dealers in Fustian" who were busy building castles in air, while the *General Advertiser* argued that the American gazettes were now far more accurate than their London counterparts. At best, it was believed the journal that was "Published by Authority" could be counted upon to deliver only a highly biased version of affairs in America; even editors loyal to the North ministry occasionally found it necessary to criticize the "absurd" reports carried in the *Gazette*.

Yet, however untrustworthy these official reports, they eventually proved to be more nearly accurate than the conflicting information that appeared in London's other publications. One letter writer declared, in May, 1775, that the daily accounts in the public newspapers were so little founded in truth that not one article in twenty could in the least be depended on. Three months later another wrote that not one account in ten could be relied upon. Despite this reputed improvement in so brief a period, wild conjectures continued to appear during the war years. An unidentified correspondent, commenting to the *St. James's Chronicle* on the most absurd rumors propagated by the Ministry—the conditions of hunger that led the American troops to eat one another, the Washington-Mrs. Gibbons tale, and the murder of the American Commander by his own sentinels—concluded that of the many advantages derived by England from the American war, "the great improvement in the Art of political Lying is not the least considerable." So long as accounts of this kind flooded the newspapers and magazines and so long as both sides accused one another of inventing these accounts, the *London Gazette* could be used to advantage by all editors. The Ministry's prints adhered closely to its official accounts of the proceedings in America, while the Opposition press assumed that anything printed in the "Royal Lying Gazette" was often far from the truth. *Gentleman's Magazine*, studying scores of "spurious accounts" of the war that were circulating throughout England, accurately concluded in late 1777 that it was no easy matter to distinguish truth from falsehood. . . .

The Ministry vs. the Opposition

Although on the offensive editorially, the Opposition feared being placed on the defensive legally. If an editor was brought before the bar by the Government, the Opposition immediately closed ranks and supported him, for they knew that if one were successfully attacked, the others might well be next. For this reason only, Henry Bate, before going to jail, took satisfaction in announcing that William Parker, printer of the *General Advertiser* and one of Bate's worst tormentors, was, in 1779, sentenced to Newgate for one year for contempt of Lords. Parker was convicted because of his acerbic comments in a special handbill that defended the acquittal of the Whig admiral, Augustus Keppel, who was court-martialed for alleged negligence in combat with French fleets during the summer of 1778. Parker, whose newspaper columns regularly contained attacks upon the Government and its subsidized press, was certain that his prosecution stemmed directly from these attacks, and he continued to give the Ministry no peace. After converting his cell into an editorial office, he managed the *General Advertiser* from Newgate. In February, 1780, while still in prison, Parker vigorously supported the crusade for the passage of Sir George Savile's motion to compel the Government to produce its pension lists. The *Morning Post*, as expected, opposed the bill. The *General Advertiser* used two full pages to list the name of every man who helped defeat this motion "in order to distinguish who are placemen, contractors, pensioners, etc.," and Parker's attacks upon the Ministry and its "prostitute morning paper" became still more pronounced. So long as he was allowed to write for his own newspaper from his cell, his imprisonment was indeed a hollow victory for the Government.

On March 20, 1780, Parker's *General Advertiser*, still boasting of its extensive and increasing sale, absorbed the insolvent and anti-Ministry *Public Ledger*. Thomas Brewman, in his final statement as editor and publisher of the *Ledger*, affirmed that he had "tried to destroy the corrupt administration," and he now believed he could help do so more effectively by serving on the staff of a larger, more influential publication. Brewman was convinced that Parker had succeeded in making the *General Advertiser* one of the most important Opposition journals in England.

In spite of all efforts by the Ministry, the press was as hostile to the Government in 1781 as it had been five years earlier. Although the *Morning Herald* had given the Tories some additional strength, no other pro-Government publications were undertaken during the American Revolution, and only one Opposition publication came over to the Government. William Woodfall's *Morning Chronicle*, which previously had balanced its paragraphs in such a way as to demonstrate that, while not wishing the American cause well, it was opposed to the Ministry that appeared to be blundering into a defeat in America, threw its support in mid-1778 behind the Ministry, once France became the major enemy. Its columns were always open, however, to hostile opinions. In summing up his father's position, William Woodfall, Jr., wrote that he was "a friend to government and a moderate man in politics." The Opposition press never forgave the *Morning Chronicle* for deserting its ranks. By 1781 the abuse that had been reserved for the *Morning Post* and the *Morning Herald* was heaped also upon the *Morning Chronicle*.

Unfortunately for the King's friends, the London press, adequately supported by rising circulation and advertising revenues, was not for sale. And this fact did not augur well for the Ministry of George III.

Benjamin Franklin and the Development of the United States

Robert M. Crunden

Benjamin Franklin is one of the central figures in early American history. His involvement in the American Revolution comes late in his life, but his role in the intellectual development of revolutionary America was pivotal. Robert Crunden is a professor of history at the University of Texas at Austin and an authority on American culture.

In 1723 a rebellious young newspaper apprentice named Benjamin Franklin stole away from his job in Boston and went to Philadelphia to make his way in the world. His success and his ability to convey that success in words made him a legend long before his death, the first American genuinely to symbolize to Europeans the possibilities of human development in America. Franklin's departure conveniently dates the decline of Boston as an intellectual center of first importance and his intellectual maturity around 1740 marks the start of the Age of Franklin in Philadelphia. His personal connection between Boston and Philadelphia also usefully connects those two cities as twin centers of the early American Enlightenment. A man could be enlightened in Boston, for the roots of enlightenment were certainly there. But one could be genuinely liberated in Philadelphia.

The Enlightenment in Europe and America shared many attitudes. Educated men revolted against the irrationality and violence of post-Reformation Europe and stressed the way human beings could become more and more perfect through the use of their reason to improve society. They in-

Excerpted from Robert M. Crunden, *A Brief History of American Culture* (New York: Paragon House, 1994). Copyright ©1994 by Paragon House. Reprinted by permission of the publisher.

sisted that God need not be as inscrutable and unknowable as many Christians believed and that the scientific study of nature would reveal the truth about religious questions. Kings and priests did not deserve the respect of mankind unless they could communicate clearly the rational bases for their actions; personal whim no longer seemed a rational way of conducting church or state. Freedom, knowledge, and humanitarianism all become touchstones: people should be free, they should use their freedom to acquire knowledge and they should use that knowledge to improve society.

In Europe, Enlightenment thinking tended to be a private affair of drawing room and personal correspondence: any outspoken attack upon a European monarch could result in censorship, exile, or prison. In America, the king was far away and so was his bishop. Local clergy, businessmen, academics, and professional men were often quite publicly enlightened; the Enlightenment and the establishment were often coextensive and puritan preachers the first to proclaim many new ideas to their literate congregations. The bulk of the citizenry might remain evangelical and only vaguely aware of these currents, but just as Thomas Jefferson and Aaron Burr could share the same presidential ticket, so evangelicals and secular leaders could share similar values and goals if with quite different emphases. Public figures wrote the Declaration of Independence and the Constitution, not prisoners or members of a discontented intelligentsia.

America was also more practical and less abstract in its Enlightenment. Europeans like Isaac Newton, Francis Bacon, and John Locke had done most of the technical thinking necessary for religious and political reform and so the extensive, abstract controversies of the European Enlightenment never made much of an impact in America. Americans perceived English taxation and military intervention as catalytic acts and did little original thinking until forced to justify their rebelliousness after 1763. Within a remarkably short time they produced the political science that helped change the way multitudes far away from America viewed their own government.

In its turn, America helped Europeans locate their myths.

Utopian fantasies needed a plausible place to take root and America was the playground of the European imagination. It had no real aristocracy or monarch and by the middle eighteenth century no established church comparable to European establishments. Americans could grow up to lead rational, virtuous lives because their social environment did not oppress them. In this context Benjamin Franklin played his key role. To countless Europeans who had never met an American and who would never see the country, Franklin was the embodiment of their utopian fantasies. The rustic sage, the plain-spoken man of folk wisdom, the natural man of scientific inventiveness—he was an institution, not a real person of flesh and blood. He affected Quaker expressions and a coonskin cap and played his role with the skill of a Talleyrand. He was the European intellectuals' foil against the vapidities of aristocratic life, the proof that freedom from priestcraft brought virtue and progress. When he and Voltaire finally appeared together, the Old and New World Enlightenments came together in one of those fleeting moments of aesthetic perfection in history: two wily old men, loving their own legends, acting out the public fantasy. Rationality was the great myth of the age and America supplied its own saints; even more incredible, it put them into public office.

The American Enlightenment was also far more nationalistic than the European. In Europe, philosophy, literature, and science tended to be international; nations all too often were under the domination of irrational monarchs. But America was new and free from much of this and an American could plausibly intermingle ideas about democracy, rationality, nature, a benign Deity, and his own country. America was the place where these things could happen, in fact were already happening. In this manner intellectual positions like freedom to worship, the right to trial by peers, or the right to vote became identified with an "American way," and this way took on religious sanction. To Canadians or Australians, by contrast, such ideas were not relevant. Settled largely at later times, they avoided many eighteenth-century issues. Settled often with government police, military and bureaucratic assistance, they associated freedom, prosperity, and even their own identity with Home—i.e., the Mother Country, England. Neither religion nor revolution came up in this context at all.

Franklin as a Bridge Between Boston and Philadelphia

Philadelphia made its first contributions to the creative life of the world in the natural sciences. The old "natural philosophy" was in the final stages of its evolution into "the sciences" as the modern world knows them. The first specialists in fields like botany and geology were emerging, chiefly in continental Europe. British science was somewhat laggard, but the formation of the Royal Society of London (1660) marked the beginning of serious British contributions in a systematic and organized way. The Royal Society immediately formed a Committee for Foreign Correspondence and Americans were present in significant numbers—fifty-three names appeared on the list between 1663 and 1783, many of whom had genuine scientific interests. Over this period the American contribution was to collect new data, classify it, and give it proper nomenclature. For most contributors the emphasis was on flora and fauna, with only passing attention to other areas. For example, John Winthrop, Jr. (1606–1676), although frequently elected to public office because of his famous name and diplomatic disposition, was a chemist and physician who dabbled in alchemy. Over the years he sent the Royal Society reports on maize, cornbread, and beer; on one occasion he shipped over the first hummingbird nest ever seen in the Old World, along with a report about the characteristics of this strange new creature.

Boston provided the first genuine scientific community in the colonies. Increase Mather had had a fascination for comets. Cotton Mather accumulated a decent library on science and medicine and wrote at length about the more nauseating ways to cure oneself of various ailments: *The Angel of Bethesda* has a whole chapter on ways to use urine and dung as internal specifics to cure diseases. During the Presidency of John Leverett (1708–1724), Harvard University was a center for scientific investigation. Cotton Mather, Leverett, and

William Brattle were all fellows of the Royal Society, and Mather won a secure if small place for himself in the history of medicine when he read about the practice of inoculation against smallpox in a medical journal, ignored the best medical opinion of the day, and inoculated his own children among others in the early 1720s. A later John Winthrop (1714–1779) was Hollis Professor at Harvard and the first genuinely productive scholar on its faculty, making significant contributions to the study of earthquakes and comets. None of these men felt the least conflict between their religious and their scientific ideas. For them the natural laws were as much a part of the laws of God as the covenant theology and Christians had a duty to discover those laws as an act of fealty to the Divinity. All assumed that scientific knowledge and biblical knowledge complemented each other.

Young Benjamin Franklin was certainly aware of the scientific work going on around him as a teenager in Boston, but nevertheless he found a far freer intellectual and social climate in Philadelphia. William Penn had been the second American Fellow of the Royal Society (1681), and the period of Franklin's early maturity was one in which public attendance at scientific lectures and general interest in the subject were remarkably high. Science enjoyed an enormous prestige after Isaac Newton and Francis Bacon: men were eager to discover the rationality of their natural environment, which not only encouraged someone like Franklin, it used his insights and made a hero out of him as well. When Peter Kalm, a student of Karl Linnaeus, visited America, Franklin was one of the figures he wanted to meet, and some American contributions appeared in the *Systema Naturae* (1735). More typical of American emphases, John and William Bartram developed their famous botanical garden, the kind of investigation that seemed the most productive of insights, given the state of botany at that time.

Franklin seemed an improbable figure to give the age its name. He was the son of an elderly candlemaker who intended him for the church. Instead, Franklin early felt an aversion to both religious controversy and ceremony. As an apprentice on the *New England Courant* of his brother James, he watched his brother experience the attacks of the Mather forces on the smallpox issue and even serve a term in jail for offending the magistrates. Once safely started upon his career in Philadelphia, Franklin began his famous Junto, a kind of social club that met on Friday nights at local taverns for thirty years to discuss public questions. In time the Junto organized a circulating library and Franklin became the official printer of Pennsylvania. A practical interest in science went along with a curiosity that came in the years 1745–1752, when he pursued his work in thunder gusts and electricity and made his famous experiments with kites. His invention of the lighting rod received recognition in Europe and when Europeans replicated his electrical experiments he became well-known and even translated into German and Italian. Immanuel Kant referred to him as the new Prometheus who had stolen fire from the heavens. Simultaneously with his conduct of many other interests, he pursued experiments with ants and memory, weather, cyclones, agriculture, the Franklin stove, and light.

In the 1750s he became deeply involved in public affairs, reorganizing the postal network and making a beginning toward a more rational and unified colonial organization. His work took him across the country and his experience made him the logical choice to be representative of the Pennsylvania Assembly in London. Franklin took the opportunity to explore Europe as well, continuing his scientific interests and experimenting in the new area of musical glasses. Oxford gave him an honorary degree. But as the political situation deteriorated in the 1760s, Franklin became the key colonial spokesman in England and his scientific interests faded under pressure of current events. An eager supporter of an English-language empire, he worked hard to reconcile the colonies and the mother country. Early in the 1770s he began work on his *Autobiography*, which despite its structural flaws and omissions became the first work of American literature to be of permanent importance—not only because the author was well-known, but also because his book so simply formulated American myths of industry, utility, and upward mobility. He returned to America to become the oldest delegate to the Second Continental Congress and then went on to France for his astonishing old age as the Sage of the New World and the embodiment of Enlightenment Man. By the time his aging eyes had led him to the invention of bifocal glasses, he was quite possibly the most famous man in the Western world.

Native American Participation in the Revolution

Colin G. Calloway

During the American Revolution, some Native American tribes fought on the British side, some on the American, and others remained neutral. Colin Calloway, the chair of the Native American Studies department at Dartmouth College, discusses the various positions that Native American tribes took during the war, and how the British and Americans tried to influence their allegiance.

In Indian country the American Revolution often translated into an American civil war. While British regulars and Continental troops fought campaigns in the East, in the backcountry—which usually meant the Indians' backyards—whites killed Indians, Indians killed whites, Indians killed Indians, and whites killed whites in guerilla warfare that was localized, vicious, and tolerated no neutrals. Dissension and disruption in Indian Councils increased as militant voices drowned out words of moderation.

In Indian country and Indian communities the outbreak of the Revolution usually generated division and confusion, not united tribal action. Some people saw in the Revolution and the promise of British support a chance to drive Americans from their lands; others hoped to keep out of it; still others volunteered to fight alongside American neighbors. Abenakis in western Maine debated night after night as to what to do now that Englishmen were killing one another. One Abenaki woman said she thought the world was coming to an end. Catawba Indians in South Carolina "were alarmed, and could not tell what to make of it." George Morgan found Indians in

the Ohio Valley "much confused and unsettled in their Resolutions" in the spring of 1776. The Spanish governor of Saint
Louis, Fernando de Leyba, told the governor of Louisiana,
Bernardo de Galvez, in the summer of 1778 that the war was
"causing a great number of Indian tribes to go from one side
to the other without knowing which side to take."

Not all Indian people were living in Indian country when
the Revolution broke out, and Indians responded to the
event as individuals, not just as tribal units. Joseph Burd
Jaquoi, a Mohegan Indian from Connecticut, had served in
the Seven Years' War and was in England on a lieutenant's
half pay when the Revolution began. He was offered a captain's commission in the British army but, he said in a later
petition to the government of Connecticut, "refused to serve
in that unnatural contest." He gave up his lieutenancy, forfeited his half pay, and returned to America. Taking up residence in North Carolina, he joined the American army to
fight against his former comrades in arms when the British
invaded the Carolinas. Other Indians also enlisted in the
American cause as individuals. "Lewis Indian" and "James
Indian" volunteered for service in New Hampshire companies in the first months of the war. "Peter Indian," a Dartmouth graduate, enlisted in a New Hampshire company to
fight Burgoyne in 1777. Others, with distinct Indian names
or with names no different from their colonial comrades,
joined up in other colonies; still others may have enlisted
with their Indian identity unrecorded.

When "this island began to shake and tremble along the
Eastern shore," the American Revolution looked very much
like an English civil war to Indian eyes. Most Indian people
seem to have regarded it as a family quarrel in which they
had no business meddling. Mohegan preacher Samson
Occom wished the whites "would let the poor Indians alone,
what have they to do with your Quarrels." British and American agents encouraged a non-involvement on the part of the
Indians in the early months of the war, when they were so-
liciting neutrality rather than support from the tribes. Before long, however, British and American, then Spanish and
French, agents began to lobby Indian peoples for their active

support, justifying their actions with the argument that if they did not employ Indians as allies, the enemy would. The Continental Congress resolved in December 1775 to call on Indians "in case of real necessity." The British likewise pleaded necessity in enlisting Indian support for the defense of Canada, and in forest warfare, where their enemies employed Indians. Where Indian support was not forthcoming, British and Americans naturally preferred to factionalize tribes than to see them swing into the enemy camp. . . .

Holding Indian Allegiance

Winning Indian allegiance was one thing; retaining it amidst shifting fortunes of war and competing diplomacies required constant attention to gift giving, protocol, and local chiefs. In the spring of 1777, British agent William Caldwell warned the Senecas not to "regard anything the Bigknife [Americans] might say to them for tho he had a very smooth Oily Tongue his heart was not good." Two years later, American commander Daniel Brodhead warned the Shawnees that the British would tell them fine stories but had come three thousand miles only "to rob & Steal & fill their Pockets." As long as Detroit remained in British hands, securing the support or at least the neutrality of the French and Indian inhabitants of the Illinois country was vital to the American war effort. Pulled between British and American agents, many tribes in the Wabash and Illinois country "got divided among themselves part for us others for the English," recalled George Rogers Clark. Having won many of the Indians over by his hard-line diplomacy, Clark realized that they "required great attention to keep the Flame from cooling too soon."

Discourse and discord were part of the normal process by which Indian societies reached consensus. However, the issues raised by the Revolution were such that consensus could not always be reached. The divisions of colonial society that John Adams summarized as one-third patriot, one-third loyalist, and one-third neutral were replicated with numerous variations in countless Indian communities in North America. As elsewhere on the frontier, the pressures imposed by the Revolution revealed existing fissures as well as creating new ones. Mohawk and Onondaga speakers asked Congress to ignore the actions of individuals who went against the consensus of the Iroquois League. In 1779 the Delawares asked Congress to distinguish between their nation as a whole, which was still friendly, and the actions of a few individuals who, like the Tories in the states, sided with the British and had been obliged to leave the nation. . . .

Differing Reactions to the Americans

Some of the groups most consistently hostile to the Americans were actually bands composed of what Americans termed "renegade" warriors from various tribes. One of the first communities to wage war against the Americans was Pluggy's Town on the Oletangy River, where Chippewas, Wyandots, and Ottawas joined the Mingoes (Ohio Iroquois), and where Americans found it was often "difficult to tell what Nation are the Offenders." Like the Mingo chief Logan, Pluggy had good reason for his hostility, having returned from peace talks after Dunmore's War to find "his blood relations lieing dead" at the hands of Virginians. Pluggy's Mingoes caused consternation among Americans and among neighboring tribes who blamed them for corrupting their young men and threatening to embroil them all in war. The Americans wanted to destroy Pluggy's Town but held off for fear they would spark a general Indian war.

The League of the Iroquois or Six Nations—the confederacy of Mohawks, Oneidas, Tuscaroras, Onondagas, Cayugas, and Senecas that stretched across upper New York State—had managed to maintain a pivotal position in North American affairs by preserving formal neutrality and essential unity of action in previous conflicts, but was unable to do so in this one. According to British agent Daniel Claus, the sudden death of superintendent Sir William Johnson on the very eve of the Revolution left the Iroquois "scattered like a flock of helpless sheep." Presbyterian missionary Samuel Kirkland heard many Indians say that "they never knew a debate so warm & contention so fierce to have happened between these two Brothers, Oneidas & Cayugas, since the commencement of their union."

In 1775 the Oneidas and other Iroquois took a neutral stance, but two years later they were killing each other. Mary Jemison, an adopted white captive living with the Senecas, recalled how her people returned from meeting the Americans at German Flats, where they had pledged their neutrality late in the summer of 1775, "well pleased that they could live on neutral ground, surrounded by the din of war, without being engaged in it." But in 1777, after pestilence struck Onondaga, the central council fire was ritually extinguished for the first time in the league's history, and civil war erupted. Jemison said the British invited Iroquois warriors "to come and see them whip the rebels" at the siege of Fort Stanwix, but instead of "smoking and looking on, they were obliged to fight for their lives" in the bloody battle at Oriskany. The memory of the hand-to-hand fighting haunted Seneca chief Blacksnake into his old age: "There I have Seen the most Dead Bodies all it over [sic] that I never Did see, and never will again[.] I thought at the time the Blood Shed a Stream Running Down on the Descending ground During the afternoon." The Senecas suffered heavy losses, and Jemison remembered the "sorrow and distress" in her community after the battle. Pro-British warriors burned Oneida crops and houses in revenge; Oneidas retaliated by burning Mohawk homes. The Oneidas themselves split into factions; most supported the Americans, but some joined the British. The Tuscaroras also supported the Americans, whereas the Cayugas lent their weight to the crown. The Onondagas struggled to maintain neutrality until American troops burned their towns in 1779. For the Iroquois, the Revolution was a war in which, in some cases literally, brother killed brother. . . .

A Total War

The American Revolution was not only a civil war for many Indian peoples; it also amounted to a total war in Indian country. Indian and non-Indian nations were at war, on the brink of war, or arranging alliances in expectation of war. American history has paid little attention to the impact of this war on the Indians' home front. Operating out of De-

troit and Niagara, the British utilized Indian allies and terror tactics to demoralize American frontier settlements, but
Indian country suffered more than its share of killing, rav-
aging, and destruction. George Morgan recognized that
whatever policies the United States might try to pursue toward the Indians, "many persons among ourselves wish to
promote a War." Indian leaders appealed to American leaders to "restrain your foolish young Men," just as whites appealed to Indian chiefs to restrain their warriors, with
equally ineffective results. American commissioners warned
Creek headmen in 1777 "We look to you to stop the killing,
or our own beloved men & warriors will not hinder a just retaliation." The chiefs could do little and retaliation begat retaliation. According to Richard White, "Murder gradually
and inexorably became the dominant Indian policy" as backcountry settlers took the law into their own hands, killing
mediation chiefs and noncombatants, and undermining the
work of George Morgan and the policies of Congress.

When war came, American strategy—like that of the
French and the British before them, and of the Spanish in
dealing with recalcitrant tribes west of the Mississippi at this
time—aimed to carry the war into Indian country, destroy
Indian villages, and burn Indian crops late in the season
when there was insufficient time for raising another crop before winter. Despite the adoption of commercial hunting and
the addition of fruit, potatoes, cattle, pigs, and domestic fowl
to their diet and their economy, the sacred "three sisters" of
the Iroquois—corn, beans, and squash—remained the staff
of life for many woodland Indians. Trader James Adair said
corn was an Indian people's "chief produce and main dependence." Corn was also at the core of many tribes' spiritual
well-being: Cherokees recalled the mythical female origins
of their agriculture in the story of Selu, a woman whose
name means "corn"; and annual Green Corn ceremonies en-
sured ritual purification of the community. Like the buffalo
in Plains Indian culture and economy, corn for eastern
woodland Indians was the basis of life and prosperity but was
also an Achilles' heel, providing enemy armies with a target
that could be hit time and again with devastating effect. In

the Revolution, American armies waged war against Indian cornfields. Daniel Brodhead maintained that marching a thousand men into Indian country was a more effective means of protecting the frontier than employing three times that number as garrisons. General Armstrong agreed that carrying the war to the Indians' homes and families had an adverse effect on their morale: the Indians might flee their towns, "but their huts and cornfields must remain, the destruction whereof greatly affects their old men, their women, and their children." American troops and militia tramped through the Susquehanna, the Allegheny, the Scioto, Miami, and Tennessee valleys, leaving smoking ruins and burned cornfields behind them. As John Shy has pointed out, colonial military forces were used less often for protection of settlements than for exacting retribution and retaliation.

American soldiers and militia matched and sometimes exceeded their Indian adversaries in the use of terror tactics. George Rogers Clark informed Fernando de Leyba, lieutenant governor of Spanish Illinois in November 1778, that "the Absolute orders of Congress to the Army now in Indian Country is to Shew no mercy to those that have been at war against the States." Clark believed no punishment was too great for Indians and those who fought alongside them. He declared that "to excel them in barbarity was and is the only way to make war upon Indians and gain a name among them," and carried his policy into grisly effect at Vincennes by binding and tomahawking Indian prisoners within sight of the besieged garrison. William Henry Drayton and Andrew Williamson of South Carolina advocated that captured Indians become the slaves of the captors but the legislature refused, fearing Indian retaliation for such a precedent. Since Indian prisoners brought no reward, soldiers killed them for their scalps. Captain William Moore's contingent captured three Cherokees in their campaign against the Middle towns in 1776. Moore argued that the prisoners should be kept under guard until Congress approved their sale, but he was obliged to give in to the demands of his men since "the Greater Part swore Bloodily that if they were not Sold for Slaves upon the Spot, they would kill and Scalp them Immediately." South Carolina paid £75 for male scalps; Pennsylvania offered $1,000 for every Indian scalp. Kentucky militia who invaded Shawnee villages dug up graves to scalp corpses. . . .

The War in Indian Country

Even when the war was not fought on the Indians' home ground, it produced reverberations in Indian communities. News of battles lost and won spread far and wide through Indian villages, often faster than British and American agents could convey or contain it. Rebels and redcoats regularly attributed news adverse to their cause as the false singing of "bad birds." News of Henry Hamilton's capture by George Rogers Clark in 1779 reached Wabasha and the Sioux as they were on route to fight for the British, and stopped them short at Prairie du Chien. Likewise, news of Clark's attack on the Shawnee villages in 1782 reached the Indians at Detroit and Niagara before the British had it. British attempts to suppress news of Burgoyne's defeat and the Peace of Paris had no chance of success.

Whether warriors fought on their own ground or in some distant campaign, communities suffered from their absence. Men who fell in battle were not only warriors; they were "part-time soldiers" who were also husbands, fathers, sons, and providers. Warriors who were off fighting could not hunt or clear fields; women who were forced to flee when invasion threatened could not plant and harvest. Indians still tried to wage war with the seasons: warriors preferred to wait until their corn was ripe before they took up the hatchet, and according to one observer "quit going to war" when hunting season came. But war now dominated the activities of the community and placed tremendous demands on the people's energy at the expense of normal economic and social practices. Even before Sullivan's campaign,[1] there were food shortages in Iroquois longhouses. British Indian agent John Butler reported in September 1778, "As the

1. In the fall of 1779, General John Sullivan led his famous expedition into Iroquois country on a campaign of destruction that burned forty towns, an estimated 160,000 bushels of corn, and "a vast quantity of vegetables of every kind."

Young Men were already either out at War, or ready to go with me, they had nothing to subsist upon but the remains of last Years Corn which was near expended, their hunting being neglected." A month later the Mohawks were getting sick from eating nothing but salt meat. At a time when the need for food increased greatly, Indians could not cultivate the usual quantities of corn and vegetables, and what they did grow was often destroyed before it could be harvested.

Crops also suffered from natural causes in time of war. The late 1770s marked the beginning of a period of "sporadically poor crops" among southeastern tribes. Partial failure of the Creek corn crop in 1776 produced near famine at a time when the influx of Cherokee refugees placed additional demands on food supplies, and there was "an absolute Famine" in the Creek nation in July 1778. Choctaw crops failed in 1782, increasing the people's reliance on deer hunting. A bushel of corn sold for $8 in the Wyandot towns in the winter of 1781–2, and Moravian Indians in exile around Sandusky had nothing to eat but wild potatoes and the meat of their dead cattle. As the famine deepened, many Moravian Delawares returned to their homes on the Tuscarawas in search of food, where they fell victim to American frontiersmen. Famine returned to the Ohio Valley in 1784. Hunting became vital to group survival but fewer hunters were available, fighting scared away game, and hunting territories could be perilous places in time of war. There was never enough game to support the unusually large concentrations of Indians at refugee centers like Niagara, Sandusky, and Detroit. . . .

Indian Communities Changed by War

The revolutionary era intensified political changes in Indian communities. As in colonial society, voices of moderation were often drowned out by the clamor of the militants. Endemic warfare and outside influences continued the elevation of war chiefs, who traditionally exercised only temporary authority, over the village chiefs who looked after the concerns of the community in normal circumstances. The abnormal was now normal, and war captains like Pipe and White Eyes of the Delawares, Mohawk Joseph Brant, and Dragging

Canoe among the Cherokees spoke with an increasingly loud voice in their nation's councils. Tenhoghskweaghta, an Onondaga chief, explained: "Times are altered with us Indians. Formerly the Warriors were governed by the wisdom of their uncles the Sachems but now they take their own way & dispose of themselves without consulting their uncles the Sachems—while we wish for peace and they for war." Oneida chiefs lamented, "We Sachems have nothing to say to the Warriors. We have given them up for the field. They must act as they think wise." War and disease aggravated the situation. Cha-ha, a Wea war chief, told Henry Hamilton in a council at Detroit in 1778, "I am a War Chief, but speak on Wampum that came from our Village Chiefs or those remaining of them, for you know the loss we have met with." New leaders like Pluggy and Dragging Canoe attracted followings that cut across village, tribal, and kinship ties. Older chiefs complained increasingly that they could not control their young men—or as was often the case in the polyglot communities created by the Revolution, control somebody else's young men. . . .

Migrations increased dramatically in the revolutionary era. Seasonal movements for social or subsistence purposes now gave way to flight from the horrors of war. Some groups migrated rather than be caught up in the fighting. Communities splintered and reassembled, sometimes amalgamating with other communities beyond the reach of American armies. Refugees flooded into Niagara, Schenectady, Detroit, Saint Louis, Saint Augustine, and Pensacola; Iroquois Loyalists moved to new homes on the Grand River in Ontario. Hundreds of refugee Indians drifted west of the Mississippi and requested permission to settle in Spanish territory. Spanish officials at Saint Louis complained that visiting Indians ate them out of house and home and did not even allow them time to sleep. Migrations produced chain reactions far across Indian country. Displaced peoples from the eastern woodlands pushed into the hunting territories of Osages and Pawnees, who then pressured the ranges of the Comanches, who in turn pushed against Apaches and the northern frontier of Spanish settlement. Leaving familiar sites took an emotional as well as an economic toll.

Nor were Indian people the only migrants in Indian country. Micmacs in Nova Scotia suffered from the inroads of Loyalist settlers fleeing the Revolution to the south; Loyalists poured into West Florida, sometimes via Upper Creek villages; English settlers from Natchez who rebelled against Spanish rule in 1781 fled reprisals and took refuge in Chickasaw country.

Escalating warfare and its concomitant economic disruption reached even into ritual and ceremonial life. Eastern woodland Indians followed a social and ceremonial calendar tied to the rhythm of the seasons. Traditional warfare could be waged when the season was appropriate, and in 1778 the Creeks frustrated the British by refusing to take the warpath until after the Green Corn Ceremony. But the endemic warfare of the Revolution threw many traditional religious practices and sacred observances into disarray. Not only did the ancient unity of the Iroquois League crumble, but many of the ceremonial forms that expressed that unity were transformed or lost altogether. Preparatory war rituals were neglected or imperfectly performed. The Cayuga leader Kingageghta lamented in 1789 that a "Great Part of our ancient Customs & Ceremonies have, thro' the Loss of Many of our principal men during the War, been neglected & forgotten, so that we cannot go through the whole with our ancient Propriety." The traditional Cherokee year was divided into two seasons, with the winter reserved for war, and returning warriors underwent ritual purification before reentering normal village life. Now war was a year-round activity, and Chickamauga communities existed on a permanent war footing. In addition, the Cherokees' six major religious festivals of the year became telescoped into one—the Green Corn Festival. Cherokees remembered the 1780s as marking the end of the old ways. The loss of sacred power threatened the Indians' struggle for independence and, according to historian Gregory Dowd, Indian resistance movements of the revolutionary and postrevolutionary era drew strength from the recognition that they "could and must take hold of their destiny by regaining sacred power." Indians in the new republic sought to recover through ritual, as well as through war and politics, some of what had been lost.

The American Army: Two Theories of Leadership

Lawrence Delbert Cress

The American army was small, poorly supplied, and, on many occasions, poorly led. Two exceptional men, George Washington and Charles Lee, were able to make a difference in the army's success. In this excerpt, Cress compares the leadership styles of Washington and Lee. A military historian, Lawrence Delbert Cress's works include *Dispatches from the Mexican War*, a collaboration with George Wilkins Kendall.

The conflicting views held by Charles Lee and George Washington about the kind of military establishment needed to accomplish the goals of the Revolution mirrored the ideological tensions that pervaded American attitudes toward the military during the war years. Both men were committed to the establishment of a republican society in America. Nevertheless, their dissimilar views concerning the nature of citizenship and the structure of society necessary to preserve republican civil and political liberties produced very different critiques of the revolutionary military establishment.

Lee's Views on the Military

When the Continental army was organized in June 1775, Lee received one of six major general commissions. Like the other ranking officers in the nascent American army, he was well acquainted with the training, tactics, and discipline that made the British army so effective. What made Lee different, though, was his deep suspicion of military professionalism—a suspicion derived from a personal association with the English Whig opposition to George III. Even the "courtly" Blackstone, he had reminded the colonists in 1774, believed that "freedom cannot be said to exist, or she exists so lamely, as scarcely to deserve the name," in a country where military camps, barracks, and fortresses separated the daily duties of the citizenry from the responsibility to bear arms. With the support of men of "the first distinction and property," Lee was convinced that the American states could field an army both more "formidable against the external enemy, and less dangerous to their fellow-citizens" than a body of professional soldiers. The army he had in mind would be drawn directly from the state militias.

Lee opposed the use of bounties to attract soldiers into the army for the duration of hostilities. The republic risked losing its freedom to the very force charged with its defense if Americans did not have "virtue enough to submit to laws which obliged every citizen to serve his turn as a soldier." Enlistment incentives and extended service discouraged the cultivation of martial arts among most of the citizenry, while they promoted the development of a "distinct profession" of arms composed of "the most idle, vicious, and dissolute" part of society. Republican society, argued Lee, depended on the preservation of the classical relationship between property, citizenship, and the right and responsibility to bear arms. Every citizen should serve in the militia, and there should be no provision for substitution, short of infirmity. Active military duty should be rotated among the citizenry and limited to no more than two months annually. Lee did not believe that the rotation of military service would hinder military effectiveness, because only the most rudimentary tactics were necessary for soldiers "drawn from their ploughs." "Marching in front, retreating and rallying by their colours and all firing at marks" were the only tactics required of a republican army, and those skills could be learned at locally organized, weekly training sessions for soldiers not on active duty.

Lee's plan for a citizen militia was influenced by Machiavelli and was reminiscent of proposals developed by John Toland and Andrew Fletcher, but his insights into tactics were influenced by the French military theorist Marshal

Maurice Comte de Saxe. Tactical simplification was part of Saxe's plan to give France a national army built upon a compulsory five-year military obligation for persons from "all conditions in life," the elimination of the cumbersome ornamental garb in favor of more functional and durable clothing, and the use of more flexible strategies designed to take full advantage of both the tactical possibilities of cavalry and artillery and the collective personality, "l'imbecilité du coeur," of the troops in the field. Saxe's plan had truly revolutionary implications for the military order of western Europe and was destined to undermine the hierarchical order of European society. The full significance of his ideas awaited the declaration of the *levée en masse*—an event Condorcet considered to have transferred the theoretical equality of democracy to the reality of life. Lee, however, did not embrace the social implications of the tactical system that he appropriated. His perception of an ideal republican society was profoundly conservative and fundamentally premodern, and would have been acceptable to political theorists ranging from Harrington to Burgh.

An analysis of Lee's plan for a military colony makes that clear. Each of the ten thousand men in the colony would hold property ranging from two hundred acres for rank-and-file militiamen to twenty-five hundred acres for colonels. "For the sake of order," reasoned Lee, "there should . . . be some difference of property in the different classes of men." He clearly did not foresee his colony becoming a model for frontier democracy. Nor did he expect the colony to become a haven for land speculators or ambitious merchants. An agrarian law would restrict property ownership to five thousand acres, preventing any small faction of landholders from imbalancing the civil order. Commerce would have no place, either. Commercial employment was forbidden because it "must emasculate the body, narrow the mind, and in fact corrupt every true republican and manly principle" essential to the virtue of free citizens. The "effeminate and vile" commercial occupations necessary for the functioning of even this noncommercial society were left to the employment of women. The male citizens of the colony would devote themselves to farming, hunting, and the martial arts. The militia and the militiamen, then, became not only a military alternative to a standing army but also the reflection of a social system qualitatively different from the emerging complex commercial societies of Britain and Europe which looked to a professional military for their defense.

Washington's Troops

Whereas Lee sought a return to the kind of society that Adam Smith believed was compatible with the deployment of citizen-soldiers, Washington considered the American republic to be more like the modern, commercial society that Smith had described as unable to support a citizen army. Washington had not read *Wealth of Nations;* nevertheless, he analyzed American military requirements in terms reminiscent of Smith's defense of a permanent and professional military establishment. Advocates of the citizen-soldier believed that a commitment to the common good would bring the militia out and keep it in the field, but, argued Washington, they simply misunderstood the motives of those willing to do military service in the eighteenth century. He contended that few men, even in a republic, would serve disinterestedly and that fewer still could identify their interests with a low-paying army. This fact explained the mediocrity and ineptitude plaguing the American officer corps and the difficulty of finding recruits for the enlisted ranks. To attract the men of character and stature necessary for an effective officer corps, military service had to be made economically advantageous. National interests had to be linked to personal interests, and that meant a pay scale high enough to make the officer "independent of every body but the State he Serves." The economic interests of the enlisted soldier also had to be entwined with the military success of the republic. Virtue alone had proven and would continue to prove inadequate to inspire men to suffer the hardships of military campaigns. But soldiers would be willing to serve, even for the duration of hostilities, if ample rewards in the form of land and money were provided.

Washington looked to higher bounties to resolve the

chronic manpower shortages faced by the American army, but he also believed that only bounties would provide the long-serving regulars that would ensure the discipline and order necessary for successful military campaigns. Militia soldiers were civilians first and soldiers second. They might be familiar with the manual of arms, but soldiering remained only a part of their role in society. Their ties with civil society also left militiamen ill prepared for the hardships of camp life and the discipline required for effective military operations. Those factors alone explained why citizen-soldiers were no match for trained regulars. Soldiering was a demanding craft, argued Washington, requiring skills and training attainable only through long and continuous service. Only when the republic separated soldiering from the other responsibilities of citizenship could it be assured of winning its independence from Great Britain.

Washington, of course, was turning upside down the radical Whig claim that the militiaman's greatest strength lay in his dual role as citizen and soldier. But for Washington, the nuances of political autonomy and economic independence were of little importance compared with the need to defeat the hardened British regulars on the battlefield. Only a victorious army could guarantee republicanism in America. His concern was for an efficient and dependable military force, and he concluded, as had the moderate Whigs, that an army composed of long-serving regulars was not only compatible with but necessary for the preservation of civil and political liberties in a free society.

The Revolutionary Army

Washington's analysis of the republic's military needs suggested that neither the social nor the military theory of classical republicanism was appropriate to the environment that spawned the American Revolution. Citizen-soldiers called from the plow and motivated by public virtue may have served the ancient republics, but only an appeal to self-interest could bring out the long-serving regulars required to ensure military victory in the modern world of military professionalism and economic specialization.

Certainly private interest had proven more important than public virtue during the initial year of hostilities. The emotional and ideological fervor that brought the militia into the field in the aftermath of Lexington and Concord had not lasted the winter campaign of 1775. After serving well at Bunker Hill, the militia's performance steadily deteriorated. Hopes for creating an army of citizen-soldiers drawn from the newly reorganized state militias all but collapsed after militiamen left Montgomcry's army stranded at the gates of Quebec when their enlistments expired.

By the summer of 1776 Congress was well on its way toward creating a military establishment that placed a premium on military expertise, avoided the use of militiamen whenever possible, and relied extensively on enlistment bonuses and bounties to fill the ranks of the chronically undermanned American army. Even John Adams was convinced that the states could not "reasonably hope to be a powerful, prosperous, or a free People [without] a permanent Body of Troops." "Indeed," wrote William Ellery of Rhode Island, "the liberties of this Country . . . cannot be established but by a large standing Army."

During the fall of 1776 Congress substantially increased enlistment bonuses, lengthened Continental enlistments to three years or the duration of the war, and adopted articles of war explicitly patterned after the British model. A year later it created the office of inspector general with duties fashioned after the "practice of the best disciplined European armies." There were those, including Charles Lee, Samuel Adams, James Warren, Benjamin Rush, and one "Caractacus," who believed that the states were exhibiting "too great a propensity . . . to trust the defence of our country to mercenary troops." But a majority of the state delegations in Congress, including such important individuals as Thomas Jefferson, John Adams, and Robert R. Livingston, accepted the principle that success on the battlefield in an age of military complexity and sophistication required trained, experienced, and disciplined troops. Fifteen months of military disappointment, caused in part by the untimely departure of militia soldiers, could justify no other conclusion. At the same time, Congress recognized that the experience and discipline necessary for victory against the professional army of Great Britain could be had only by offering significant remuneration, conceding that the eighteenth-century soldier was motivated by interest and not virtue, whether he was an American patriot or a Hessian dragoon.

The states, too, abandoned the citizen army that they had once considered "the natural strength and only stable security of a free government." After appeals to public virtue failed to produce a continuous supply of willing citizen-soldiers, they turned to the poor and disfranchised to meet state and continental manpower needs. The unmarried sons of farmers and artisans, transient laborers, newly freed or delinquent indentured servants, and even slaves were urged, induced, and compelled into military service. South Carolina designated "all idle, lewd, disorderly men, who have no battalions or settled place of abode, or no visible lawful way or means of maintaining themselves and their families, all sturdy beggars, and all strolling or straggling persons . . . liable and obliged to serve in one of the Continental regiments of this state." Maryland followed suit, making "every vagrant or man above 18 years of age, able bodied, and having no family, fixed battalion, or visible means of subsistence" subject to impressment for Continental army service. All the states encouraged the poor and landless to enlist with promises of land and monetary bounties that ranged from outright grants of money and acreage to tax exemptions and debt deferment. Many states also granted volunteers immunity from civil judicial proceedings. This usually meant that no land or personal property could be impounded for delinquent debts while the soldier remained in active service. Connecticut even proposed that localities use public revenues to support the families of soldiers willing to commit themselves to extended military service. Even militia drafts did not pretend to raise a citizen army. Economically secure individuals could gain military exemptions by paying fines or hiring substitutes. In many states two men could be deferred for the duration of the war if they hired a third to serve for the same period of time.

The unity of property and arms embodied in the citizen-soldier and so important to the ideological precepts of the Revolution failed to satisfy the pressing demands of military necessity, creating a major discrepancy between the theory of the Revolution and the military demands inherent in the fight for independence. Enlistees did not consider military service to be a lifelong occupation, but institutionally the army had many of the trappings of a professional, if not permanent, force. The Continental command clearly aspired to model their army after the professional forces of Europe. Terms of enlistment were designed to provide the republic with a single body of soldiers for the duration of the war. The lure of bounties and the promise of bonuses also reflected a recognition that self-interest, not public virtue, motivated individuals to accept the hardships of military service. Soldiers were deliberately separated from the rights and privileges enjoyed by the civilian population, and they were punished and disciplined in a manner adapted from European military codes and manuals. Certainly, no effort was made to rotate the "best men" of society into the ranks of the army. Indeed, once Congress and the states accepted the necessity of long-term enlistments, the public apparently had no trouble relegating the principal burden of military service to the poor and economically insecure.

Chapter 3

The Politics and Strategy of the American Revolution

The First Campaigns of the War

Louise and Benton Minks

The American forces in the Revolutionary War were neither well trained nor well equipped. The first campaigns included costly defeats and General Washington frequently was forced to pull his army back to safety. In this selection by authors Louise and Benton Minks the disadvantages of the first battles are clearly described. In light of these significant weaknesses, the ultimate success of the Americans is even more startling.

Problems with ill-prepared soldiers and inadequate supplies kept the colonists at a disadvantage throughout the first third of the American Revolution. There were two early campaigns, in particular, that illustrated the clumsiness and hardship of the Continental Army. The first was the 1775–76 attempt to capture Quebec and seize all of Canada, before independence had been declared; the second happened eight months later in 1776, when General Washington's plan to hold on to New York City failed.

The plan to invade Canada began to take shape with the seizure of Fort Ticonderoga in May 1775, just three weeks after the fighting at Lexington and Concord. The surprise assault on the old British fortress was a mistake, according to some delegates at the Second Continental Congress. It would give Parliament and the king just one more reason to punish the colonies. These representatives favored some kind of a compromise with their countrymen.

Other voices in the congress, however, saw the taking of Ticonderoga as an unexpected opportunity. The old fort on Lake Champlain could become a staging point for a thrust into British-owned Canada. Control of Canada would eliminate the threat of an enemy attack from the north. Even more attractive, though, was the possibility that Canada (all of eastern North America north of the St. Lawrence River) would become a 14th American colony. The great land mass would more than double the area of the 13 colonies.

Hoping that the Canadians might welcome an opportunity to support colonial resistance to the English, the Continental Congress sent a message to General Philip Schuyler, one of Washington's four major generals and the commander at Fort Ticonderoga. . . . Schuyler received the message at a time when conditions at the fort were in a shambles. Soldiers there were indifferent to discipline and order. They did not bother to keep themselves or their quarters clean, and their carelessness caused much of the food to be spoiled and valuable supplies ruined. When Schuyler first arrived at the fort, in fact, he was furious to find the guards asleep.

Second in command under Schuyler was Brigadier General Richard Montgomery, who had fought with the British in the French and Indian Wars. Montgomery, however, felt strongly about the cause of the colonies and offered his experience and intelligence to fight the British. He had proven himself a capable leader in fighting the French, but colonial troops at Ticonderoga did not feel obligated to follow a commander other than their own. . . .

Arrangements were proceeding satisfactorily until Schuyler was called to Albany, New York, on August 17, 1775, for an important meeting with prominent regional Indian chiefs. Brigadier Montgomery was left in command of the Northern Continental Army in Schuyler's absence. A scout alarmed him with the report that the British were strengthening the forts at St. Johns and elsewhere along the route that the northern army was planning to take. Furthermore, there was information that two new warships, each able to carry 20 guns, were being built in a shipyard not far from St. Johns on the Richelieu River. Montgomery decided he could not wait for orders from Schuyler, and in less than 10 days after he was given command, he was leading a force of 1,200 men on a mission to conquer half of North America for the American colonies.

Montgomery left a note for Schuyler apologizing for not

waiting to consult with him, but he indicated he had acted in his best judgment when he wrote, "If I must err, let it be on the right side." When Schuyler returned two days later, ill with a fever, he was pleased with the junior officer's decision and quickly assembled 800 additional men. They set out to join Montgomery, although Schuyler himself was forced to return to Ticonderoga because of a complete collapse of his health.

Less than a month after Montgomery launched his ambitious plan to capture Quebec and win control of Canada, Benedict Arnold received approval from General Washington to lead about 1,100 of the best riflemen he could gather to the same destination sought by the forces from Ticonderoga—Quebec. Arnold would take an eastern route through Maine, however, and meet Montgomery as he approached from the west and down the St. Lawrence River. . . .

An Unexpected Result

The Americans were counting heavily on surprising the city's supposedly weak defenders. Arnold and Montgomery were not prepared, however, for the arrival of a blinding snowstorm that began the night of December 30 and continued on into the next day. Despite the snow, Montgomery led his men into a position where they could overcome the guards and enter the city.

Unexpectedly, the guards were alert and watchful. One of them detected an advance party of the Americans moving toward the blockhouse, where a cannon was loaded and waiting. A British officer watched as the silhouettes of the invaders appeared through the driving snow and sleet. He waited until all the Americans were within sight and then fired, killing all the colonists within range of the deadly explosion of grapeshot. One of the first to fall was Brigadier General Montgomery.

Arnold's troops in the meantime were attacking the city from the east, but they had a similar experience when Arnold himself was wounded and many of his men captured. The next move of the Americans was to lay siege to the city throughout the winter of 1776 to bring about its surrender.

Although eventually 13,000 American troops were sent to Canada, there were never many more than 500 "effectives"—that is, men truly fit for fighting—against 1,600 British troops secure in Quebec. When British reinforcements arrived with the spring thaw in May, the surviving Americans slowly retreated back up the St. Lawrence. Some 5,000 Americans were left behind in Canada—dead, wounded, or captured—and another 3,000 dragged themselves back weakened by malaria, smallpox and dysentery; the last of the survivors didn't reach safety at Fort Ticonderoga until July 1776. As it happened, this was just after the Continental Congress had made its final move toward a declaration of war against Britain, but the grand plan of bringing Canada into the union of colonies had failed. . . .

Both England and America recognized that control of New York City would make a crucial difference in winning the war. New York harbor was a major gateway to Atlantic shipping, and the Hudson River connected the city to the northern frontiers. If the English occupied New York City, they would be within easy distance of New England. They would be able to move their fleet down the coast to attack any of the southern colonies, or they could use the Hudson River as a vital connector to their troops mobilizing in Canada.

After the British were forced to leave Boston in March of 1776, New York became the center of fighting for the remainder of the year. General Howe was now the supreme commander of all English forces in America, and he had the responsibility of preparing the strongest military force in the world to seize New York. For weeks after the humiliation of being driven from Boston, Howe used his time at Halifax, Nova Scotia, to make plans to attack New York. The British general was not about to move on the city until he had the assurance of an enormous advantage over the Americans in troop numbers and war supplies.

At the same time, George Washington was making plans to defend New York from attack. On March 18, 1776, the day after the evacuation from Boston, the American commander-in-chief ordered most of his men and weapons to hasten to New York. There were reports that Howe planned to invade the city by sea, using his warships. The American army was becoming a respectable force, at least in terms of size if not experience. Even with only the limited successes of Breed's Hill and the forced British evacuation of Boston, the colonists were feeling that they could manage the redcoats. General Washington did not have the same confidence. . . .

The Largest Concentrated Naval Force in History

At daybreak, on June 29, 1776, the combined fleets under Admiral Richard Howe and his brother, General William Howe, began sailing into New York harbor, one flotilla after another. Looking out his window that morning, one Patriot soldier spied "something resembling a wood of pine trees trimmed. The whole Bay was full of shipping as ever it could be. I thought all London was afloat." It was the largest concentrated naval force in British history. English warships continued to arrive during July, and by the middle of August, 32,000 British and Hessian troops were poised to strike the 20,000 Americans now in New York City.

Starting before sunrise on August 22, 1776, the British made their move. All day long, transport barges ferried about half of the invasion force from their encampment on Staten Island across New York harbor to Long Island. Fortunately for the Americans, Howe had decided to land all his troops on the southeastern shore of Long Island, *behind* the Americans on Brooklyn Heights. For in spite of his preparations, General Washington had made a serious mistake in the way he had positioned his troops. The result could have meant sure destruction of the inexperienced colonial soldiers and an early end to the war.

Washington had decided not to concentrate all his men in one place. Instead, he divided them between the two islands which are now part of New York City—Long Island and Manhattan Island. His strategy could have been a serious mistake if British General Howe had sailed up the East River and trapped the colonial forces on Long Island near Brooklyn Heights. The other half of Washington's army would remain helplessly on Manhattan, unable to cross the East River and join the Americans facing the enemy there. The battle at Brooklyn Heights began on the morning of August 27. The Americans were not prepared for the force of the attack, and they suffered heavy casualties in a crushing defeat.

In desperation, Washington concluded that he must try to salvage his remaining forces on Long Island. He must somehow get them across the East River to join the other half of his army on Manhattan Island. The only reason he was lucky enough to still have that choice was that General Howe remembered the battle at Breed's Hill very well. In spite of the major rebel defeat on Long Island, Howe halted the final attacks on Brooklyn Heights to give his men time to dig themselves in. If he had given the order to press forward and capture the trapped Americans, he might have ended the war then and there.

The prospects for Washington's evacuation plans were dismal, since the Americans had no large transport boats like the British to ferry them across the river. Washington knew, also, that he must prevent the British from discovering the attempt to evacuate. It was John Glover of Marblehead, Massachusetts, who offered a solution. An experienced mariner, Glover had been appointed by the Continental Congress to head the infant American navy. In a moment of sheer heroism, he and Israel Hutchinson of Salem devised a plan to use every available small boat they could find to ferry as many of the trapped soldiers as possible from Long Island across the East River to Manhattan. Glover's Marbleheaders and Hutchinson's 27th Massachusetts unit were coastal fishermen who knew how to manage small boats in rough waters. Throughout the night of August 29, their rugged oarsmen pulled their loaded boats through rain and blinding fog. For six hours nonstop, they crossed the East River back and forth. When the British awoke the morning of the 30th, they were astonished to find the Americans were completely gone from Brooklyn Heights. The escape had been orderly and a total success. Military strategists still regard the American escape from Long Island as a masterful achievement.

The Americans had lost Long Island, but they still had an army. Inexperience and terror had caused many of the Patriot foot soldiers to run during the battle for Long Island, but their commander, General Washington, did not show any of his own alarm. His outward steadiness and determination gave heart to his men, but there was growing uncertainty among many of the troops who had felt so confident just a few days earlier. Suddenly, the Americans faced the prospect of a long war full of bitter fighting. Long Island was not like Breed's Hill at all. In the Battle of Long Island, the British did not give the Americans time to reload their muskets. The colonists were terrified as the enemy charged with bayonets and either ran them through or sent them fleeing.

After the panic he saw in his men on Long Island, Washington was worried about how much he could count on them under fire. He faced a risky choice—to stand and fight to save New York (Manhattan) or to continue a calculated retreat. One of his advisors counseled him to abandon Manhattan immediately and escape to Westchester County just to the north of the city. Another recommendation was to burn New York and leave nothing for the British. After days of indecision, Washington finally decided to leave Manhattan on September 15, 1776, without setting fire to the city. . . .

Nathan Hale's Capture

A short time after the Americans evacuated Manhattan Island, a great fire broke out in New York, and almost one fourth of the city burned. On the day after the fire, a young American schoolteacher from Connecticut, Nathan Hale, was "taken up and dragged without ceremony to the execution post and hung up." Hale had volunteered to slip back into the city to gather information and had been imprisoned as a spy when caught making suspicious drawings. It was easy to accuse this American patriot of starting the sweeping fires in the city after the rebel retreat, and upon the gallows, Hale made his brief but memorable farewell: "I only regret that I have but one life to lose for my country."

General Washington moved his army to White Plains, New York, but he had been reluctant to abandon Manhattan Island altogether. Eventually some 4,600 American troops were positioned around Fort Washington at the northern tip of the island, a decision that led to disaster, for it was not long before the British overran the fort. Lost were priceless weapons and other supplies, but the most serious consequence was the death (53), wounding (250) or capture (2,818) of over 3,000 American soldiers. The British now held all of New York's Long Island and Manhattan Island and would keep them for the remainder of the war.

Even though the Americans had fought courageously on some days, the overall campaign to hold New York had been a slow but inevitable retreat. Washington was able to escape into New Jersey with most of his army intact by the time winter arrived, but the prospects for the Americans seemed almost hopeless. A British officer who followed the retreat was shocked that "many of the Rebels who were killed were without shoes or Stockings, without any proper shirt or Waistcoat, also in great want of blankets. They must suffer extremely." He could not imagine how the Americans could continue fighting this way, so he had every reason to believe that the American rebellion would soon end. He did not understand, however, that the Americans now had more than their pride at stake. They were fighting for a new ideal— their full independence from England.

Propaganda in America: Information and Misinformation

John C. Miller

In this selection from historian John C. Miller's work *Triumph of Freedom, 1775–1783*, the image of American revolutionary leadership is tarnished. Miller develops the thesis that both sides of the conflict engaged in misinformation about the atrocities perpetrated by the enemy. Within this discussion, a clear picture develops of the conditions of American prisoners of war and the role of the Continental Congress in condoning retaliation on British prisoners.

The British defeat in New Jersey was not wholly owing to Washington's strategy: by their conduct as conquerors the British had helped materially to undermine their position in the state. Voltaire once said that a great conqueror must be a great politician. Certain it is that the political ineptitude of the British was one of the chief causes of their failure to master the rebellion.

Sir William and Lord Howe had been magnanimous in victory: never forgetting that their chief purpose was to restore the empire, they offered, in November 1776, a free pardon to all persons in arms against the mother country who took within sixty days an oath of allegiance to the King. To them were given "protections" designed to guard them against molestation by British troops. Thus the Howes made use of every weapon, psychological as well as military, in waging war and were repaid by seeing thousands of Americans affirm their loyalty to the British Crown. The patriot cause suffered a blow almost as severe as a major military de-

Excerpted from *Triumph of Freedom, 1775–1783*, by John C. Miller. Copyright 1948 by John C. Miller. Reprinted by permission of Little, Brown and Company.

feat: farmers supplied the British army liberally with provisions; Loyalists volunteered to serve with the British army; and hundreds of rebels gave up the dubious struggle and made their peace with the conquerors.

The importance of this experiment could not easily be exaggerated: the fate of the American Revolution depended in a large measure upon what occurred in New Jersey. Had the British been able to conciliate the inhabitants, establish just and orderly government, and promise absolution from taxes imposed by the British Parliament, the Revolution would have suffered a severe setback. In this event, perhaps all the Middle colonies would have renounced the rebellion and returned to the empire.

During the entire war, the British never had a fairer opportunity of redeeming a colony than in New Jersey in 1776. Everything favored the success of Howe's experiment: the people were predominantly loyal, they rejoiced in British victories, and were eager to return to their allegiance. The reconstruction of New Jersey was, in the main, a matter of building upon the solid foundation of New Jersey Loyalism. Yet, instead of grasping this opportunity, the British turned the province into a hotbed of patriotism.

Behavior of British Troops

The work of reconciliation was largely undone by the conduct of British and Hessian troops in the conquered territory. They plundered remorselessly: instead of coming as deliverers intent upon restoring peace and order, they descended upon the countryside like a swarm of locusts. Beginning by confiscating the livestock and horses of the rebels, they graduated to the higher forms of larceny, devoting their attention to silver plate, furniture, clothing, wines, bric-a-brac and, indeed, everything of value that could be carried away. Even Loyalists armed with "protections" were not exempt from their rapacity: whatever the soldiery wanted they declared to be rebel property, and under this convenient fiction robbed friends as well as foes. "Thus," lamented a British officer, "we went on persuading to enmity those minds already undecided, and inducing our very

Friends to fly to the opposite party for protection."[1]

Taught to hate Americans as rebels, the British soldiers were anything but good-will ambassadors; toward them they practised cruelties that they would have scorned to employ against a foe whom they respected. This was a struggle in which the common Englishman was deeply moved by the passions of war: in his eyes, colonists were attempting to destroy the empire and to set themselves up as rivals of the mother country. It was inevitable, therefore, that they should have regarded Americans as treacherous parricides— "desperadoes and profligates, who have risen up against law and order in general" and who had thereby placed themselves outside the law.

As a result, what to the Americans were atrocities were sometimes to the British merely proper and wholesome chastisement. As rebels, Americans were not merely enemies of the mother country but its children who had plunged the knife into its back without provocation. Therefore, their punishment must be more severe than that meted out to foreign enemies; rebellion was an atrocity and ought to be fought with atrocities. "I think we should (whenever we get further into the country)," said Lord Rawdon in 1776, "give free liberty to the soldiers to ravage it at will, that these infatuated wretches may feel what a calamity war is.". . .

Probably the British army was neither as black as it was painted nor as guiltless as it professed to be. Howe showed much concern over the behavior of his troops and issued frequent orders against plundering. Despite all that he could do, the troops occasionally got completely out of hand. Officers who attempted to restrain them were threatened by their men as the army joined in a mad scramble for loot.[2] The Loyalists and even the British themselves admitted that

1. No doubt, the worst offenders were the women who followed the army in swarms. These harpies even stripped children of their clothing, so thorough was their pilfering. 2. At this time, there was a serious shortage of officers in the army. Howe declared that in some companies there were only two officers to three hundred men "and altho' the Men behave with great Spirit, yet, the Temptations for Plunder are so great, that it is not in the power of a few Officers to keep the Men under proper Restraint." Howe to Germain, November 30, 1776. Germain MSS., Clements Library.

the conduct of the army had been disgraceful—where Congress had made one patriot, it was said, the British army had made ten. And as for sex crimes, Lord Rawdon has left this description of the activity of the British army on Staten Island: "The fair nymphs of this isle were in wonderful tribulation, as the fresh meat our men have got here has made them riotous as satyrs. A girl cannot step into the bushes to pluck a rose without running the most imminent risk of being ravished, and they are so little accustomed to these vigorous methods that they don't bear them with the proper resignation, and of consequence we have most entertaining court-martials every day."

American Prisoners of War

Shortsightedly, the British also played into the hands of propagandists by mistreating American prisoners of war.[3] The spectacle of emaciated, haggard survivors of British jails and prison ships dragging themselves along country roads was more effective propaganda than even Thomas Paine could have coined. One look at these "poor miserable starved objects" completely disproved the claim of British generals that the atrocity stories were "a parcel of damned lies."

On board the prison ships in New York Harbor, hundreds of Americans paid the full measure of devotion to the cause of freedom. Crammed into the holds of the ships, they were confined in "a most nasty stinking Place" sometimes compared to the Black Hole of Calcutta. But the torture at Calcutta lasted only one night; aboard the prison ships it was protracted for years. Here were to be found worse horrors

3. In pursuance of the King's proclamation of August 1775, which declared Americans in arms to be traitors to the Crown, the British Ministry began by treating American prisoners as common malefactors and outlaws. They were thrown into jail and preparations were made to bring them to trial for treason. Lord George Germain and Lord Sandwich were eager to decorate Tyburn with American rebels; and many of the wounded prisoners taken by the British at Bunker Hill confidently expected to be hanged. Some Americans captured at Quebec were actually transported to England and imprisoned in Pendennis Castle as traitors. But the Ministry declined to take the next step: treason trials and executions. No American prisoners were put on trial for treason, and although many were badly mistreated, in general they were accorded the rights of belligerents. Yet it was not until 1782 that, by act of Parliament, they were officially recognized as prisoners of war rather than traitors.

than those of the battlefield: hundreds of men fighting for food and air "some swearing and blaspheming, some crying, praying and wringing their hands, and stalking about like ghosts and apparitions; others delirious . . . raving and storming; some groaning and dying—all panting for breath; some dead and corrupting." "The air was so foul at times," said a prisoner, "that a lamp could not be kept burning, by reason of which three boys were not missed until they had been dead ten days." Although the Americans sent provisions to the prisoners in New York, it was charged that the British appropriated most of the foodstuffs to their own use.

It cannot be said that the sufferings of the American prisoners in New York excited pity from the British or the Loyalists. No charity was extended these unfortunates; indeed, the Loyalists protested against the leniency shown some American officers by the British in permitting them to wear their uniforms and to walk the streets of the city after giving their parole. Some Loyalists expressed their regret that the American prisoners had not been put to death—in that event, they predicted, it would have struck "such a panic through the Continent, as would have prevented the Congress from ever being able to raise another Army."

And yet the way was open for American prisoners to gain a speedy release from these horrors by signifying their willingness to enlist in the services of the British Crown. In fact, the ordeal of the prison ships was in part deliberately contrived to induce Americans to desert their cause and go over to the British side. During the early part of the war, some British commanders made a practice of keeping American prisoners, when first captured, without food for three or four days, as a means of overcoming their reluctance to taking up arms for the King.[4]

4. Particularly in the later stages of the war, it was not necessary to resort to cruelties to induce American prisoners to enlist in the British service: the promise of higher pay and bounties sufficed. After the fall of Charleston in 1780, for example, several hundred American prisoners joined the British army and were sent to the West Indies. General Clinton was delighted with these recruits. "Such has been the Mortality from Sickness among the Troops there," he remarked, "that I do not see any other Means of recruiting them." The Continental Congress was moved to protest, alleging that these prisoners had enlisted under duress. But when it was proved that they had joined the British army voluntarily, the case was dropped.

Nevertheless, for the most part, American prisoners refused to take this easy way out of their misery. There were three hundred American prisoners at Halifax dying of jail distemper and smallpox; "yet," acknowledged Admiral Arbuthnot, "surrounded as they are by distress, they are deaf to every solicitude of taking the oath of allegiance or subscribing to any Act whereby they may be liberated." Over twelve hundred American prisoners in England stood steadfast through privation and ill treatment, refusing to the end to bear arms against their fellow Americans. Benjamin Franklin said that Englishmen "ought to glory in descendants of such virtue"; and the English Whigs, in this spirit, opened a public subscription for the relief of American prisoners in Great Britain. Edmund Burke declared that in the treatment of prisoners "the Turk, the savage Arab, the cruel Tartar, or the piratical Algerine, when compared to our ministers, might be thought humans. To the Tories, however, the courage and endurance of these American prisoners brought no rejoicing; it was apparent that men of such stern fiber were not easily conquered.

Exploiting Atrocities

Many patriots exulted in these atrocities as an effective means of weaning Americans from their love of the mother country. It was believed that if the struggle ended with Americans still harboring the least spark of affection for Great Britain, their independence would be in jeopardy: the price of liberty seemed to be eternal vigilance against the wiles of John Bull. Although the patriots told themselves that for John Bull to seek to restore himself in the graces of Americans was "like a foolish old dotard taking to his arms the bride that despises him," nevertheless they feared the charms of this old reprobate. Therefore they piled on atrocities with good will, persuaded that in so doing they did a holy work. "Let us cherish our resentments," they exclaimed. "Let us instil them into the minds of our children: and let the first lessons we teach them be, that to love liberty and to hate Englishmen is one and the same thing."

Benjamin Franklin who, had he not won greater fame as a

scientist, philosopher, statesman, and man of letters, would have deserved imperishable renown on the strength of his talents as a propagandist, skillfully dressed these atrocity stories in the guise of fact. In France, he set out to compile a "School Book" of choice atrocity stories, profusely illustrated, "in order to impress the minds of Children and Posterity with a deep sense of [British] bloody and insatiable Malice and Wickedness." On his press at Passy he printed a fictitious newspaper purporting to be a copy of the Boston *Independent Chronicle* containing an account of the cruelties perpetrated by the Indians at the orders of the British. Scalps of soldiers, farmers, women, and children—some of whom "were ript of their Mother's Bellies"—were sent to George III in order "that he may regard them and be refreshed; and that he may see our [the Indians'] faithfulness in destroying his Enemies, and be convinced that his Presents have not been made to an ungrateful People." This fabrication, widely circulated over Europe, was regarded as a genuine document. Franklin later denied that he had done injustice either to the Indians or to George III—a man who, he said, loved blood and hated Americans.

Washington took satisfaction in giving wide publicity to tales of British cruelty: they served the salutary purpose of discouraging desertion to the enemy. Upon a report being circulated that the East India Company purchased all American deserters from the Crown and sent them to the East Indies as slaves, Washington urged his friends to spread the tale, instructing them at the same time in the fine art of propaganda. It should be done, he directed, "seemingly with indifference, drop it at table before the Servants," and let the story filter down to the men.

Washington was the more inclined to make use of atrocity stories because they had the gratifying result of inducing Americans, hitherto indifferent to the patriot cause, to reach for their muskets resolved to send "the more than savage Britons . . . to Hell in the midst of their iniquities." The New Jersey farmers who had joyfully welcomed the British in 1776 were a few months later in arms against the invaders. Viewing this phenomenon, a patriot expressed the wish that the enemy would march the length and breadth of the United States. "America," he observed, "acquires strength by the progress of Howe's army—for wherever he goes he confirms the timid and the neutral characters in the cause of America, and at the same time, like a good scavenger, carries away all the Tory filth with him that lies in his way."

After the surrender of Burgoyne's army in 1777, the condition of Americans held prisoner by the British rapidly improved: the fear of wholesale retaliation and the growing recognition that fortune might not incline to the British side stimulated humanitarianism. Washington admitted that he had nothing to complain of as far as the treatment of American soldiers was concerned; but he did not fail to observe that the plight of American seamen captured by the British was becoming worse. After 1776, the prison ships were seldom used for American soldiers captured by the British, but sailors continued to be cast into those pestilential holes by the hundreds. Other captured sailors were sent to the East Indies, condemned to serve at hard labor at the British post in Senegal, or kept in close confinement in Great Britain for the duration of the war.

The danger of mistreating American prisoners of war was vividly illustrated in the case of General Prescott of the British army. Prescott captured Ethan Allen in Canada, loaded him with chains, and sent him to England to be tried as a traitor.[5] A short time later, however, Prescott was himself taken prisoner by the Americans; whereupon Washington proceeded to treat Prescott as the British general had himself dealt with Ethan Allen. Prescott spent sixteen weeks in close confinement, and at the time of his release was languishing in jail in the company of "common Malefactors, and the most notorious Villains." After being rescued from this duress, the unfortunate general was captured a second time—being taken, upon this occasion, "in bed with a Farmer's Daughter near Newport."

---

5. Ethan Allen expected to be made a martyr. "I thought to have enrolled my name in the list of illustrious *American* heroes," he said, "but was nipped in the bud." Instead of being hanged when he arrived in England, he was sent back to the United States and exchanged for a British officer held prisoner by the Americans.

American Retaliation

The Continental Congress threatened to retaliate upon British prisoners of war for the "enormities" committed against American prisoners, "at the mention of which," said Congress, "decency and humanity will ever blush." If violence was the only language Englishmen understood, Congress was prepared to conduct a war of frightfulness. In this spirit, the Americans established prison ships where British captives died by hundreds from privation and disease. In 1779, Congress ordered the imprisonment on board prison ships of all British seamen captured by Americans, and directed that they be subjected to the same treatment as that meted out to American sailors taken prisoner by the enemy. "There was not a post that arrived from America," said Lord George Germain, "which did not bring him letters filled with complaints of the barbarity experienced by prisoners at the hands of the Americans."

On both sides, prisoners of war, especially officers, were released on parole. When giving their parole, Englishmen did not always feel themselves obliged to keep faith with rebels: in their eyes, they were no more bound to keep their word than "to perform acts of common gratitude & generosity with rebels." British officers on parole were known to pay their American creditors with bills drawn on their bankers in London, and then, when given their freedom in an exchange of prisoners, to stop payment on such bills. Moreover, they frequently broke their paroles by escaping to the British lines. Over five hundred Britons captured on the high seas by John Paul Jones were given their liberty in exchange for a promise to procure the release of American prisoners in Great Britain; and yet, Franklin pointed out, not one of them carried out his promise—"so little Faith and Honour remain in that corrupted Nation." But it cannot be said that Americans showed more scruple in keeping their word.

British and German prisoners were used as farm laborers, employed in the saltworks, or, if skilled workers, sent to the gun factories. In general, the Germans were shown better treatment than were the British prisoners of war. They were given greater freedom of movement and encouraged to settle down as farmers or artisans. Frequently they were swallowed up in the country, particularly in the German-speaking sections of Pennsylvania. Sometimes they were even lionized by local society, although this privilege was usually reserved for British officers. In Fredericksburg, Virginia, for example, the Germans were made much of by the local gentry, their musical talents especially being admired. "In Europe," said one of the German officers, "we should not have got much honor by our music, but here we passed for masters. We were so overwhelmed with praise that we were really ashamed. Some of the American young gentlemen were jealous."

The First State Constitutions

Robert S. Peck

Robert S. Peck, a graduate of Yale Law School and the author of a book on the Bill of Rights, discusses the state constitutions that were drafted during the American Revolution. Once the colonies severed ties with Britain they needed a new governmental structure. The Continental Congress was empowered to develop national policy but each state desired its own political organization. These early constitutions, and especially their bills of rights, served as blueprints for the federal Constitution of 1789.

A spate of constitution writing accompanied the decision to seek independence. Thomas Jefferson wrote that creating governments conducive to liberty "is the whole object of the present controversy." The states' experiments with constitutions of their own, outlining both governmental structures and enumerated rights, provided models for the framers of the federal Constitution. In 1789, when James Madison introduced his proposal for a bill of rights, seven states had bills of rights. They were Virginia, Pennsylvania, Delaware, Maryland, North Carolina, Massachusetts, and New Hampshire. Vermont, later to be admitted as the fourteenth state, included a bill of rights in its 1777 constitution as well. Four additional states—New Jersey, Georgia, New York, and South Carolina—included rights provisions, covering guarantees of religious liberty, press freedom, and jury trial, within the body of their constitutions. Connecticut and Rhode Island continued to operate under their preindependence charters, though Connecticut added a preamble as a sort of declaration of rights. Natural rights were explicitly recognized in the declarations of seven states.

Excerpted from *The Bill of Rights and the Politics of Interpretation*, 1st ed., by Robert S. Peck, ©1991. Reprinted with permission of Wadsworth Publishing, a division of International Thomson Publishing, fax: 800-730-2215.

These early constitutional guarantees have taken on an added importance today as state courts are rediscovering their state constitutions and occasionally ruling that the rights described in these documents provide even greater protection than does the federal Constitution. The independent and sometimes earlier establishment of a state constitutional right enables state supreme courts, when they deem it merited, to attach greater reach to that right. In these instances, the U.S. Constitution is regarded as establishing a floor below which civil liberties protections cannot fall, but not affecting the ceiling to which they might rise under a more far-reaching state provision. In defending a different interpretation of state constitutional rights from that accorded under the federal Constitution, Justice Stanley Mosk of the California Supreme Court wrote that "the Bill of Rights was based upon the corresponding provisions of the first state constitutions, rather than the reverse." As a result, state supreme courts have been relying more heavily on the legislative history of sometimes identically worded state guarantees to arrive at different applications.

Enactment of a constitution at the time of independence was not the solemn, complex process we now associate with the federal Constitution. Of the eleven state constitutions written in the founding era, nine were ordinary legislative instruments that required no recourse to the people for ratification. The remaining two were promulgated by conventions, specially elected for the task of drafting a state charter.

Virginia

Virginia, the largest colony, led the movement toward written constitutions. Having called upon Congress "to declare the United Colonies free and independent states," Virginia immediately established a twenty-eight–member committee to draft a plan of government and declaration of rights. Among the committee's members were chairman Archibald Cary, George Mason, Patrick Henry, Edmund Randolph, and James Madison. Mason, in particular, was disappointed by the committee's composition, overrun as it were, he said, with "useless members." The result, he contended, would be a preoccupation with "a thousand ridiculous and impracticable proposals," resulting in a plan "formed of het[e]rogeneous, jarring and unintelligible ingredients." Mason preempted this unwelcome turn of events by proposing a plan that Randolph characterized as having "swallowed up all the rest."

Passed in convention on June 12, 1776, a month before the Declaration of Independence was issued, the Virginia Declaration of Rights began with an eloquent statement of natural-rights philosophy. It declared that

> all men are by nature equally free and independent, have cer-
> tain inherent rights, of which, when they enter into a state of
> society, they cannot, by any compact, deprive or divest their
> posterity; namely, the enjoyment of life and liberty, with the
> means of acquiring and possessing property, and pursuing
> and obtaining happiness and safety.

It is significant that the first constitutional document in the United States began with a dedication to natural rights. It served notice that these rights are not grants of any government, even one based on the consent of the people, but are instead a more fundamental and higher law that a legitimate government must recognize and protect. Moreover, because the Virginia Constitution began with a bill of rights, no more emphatic declaration could have been made of the preeminent role of rights within the system of American values.

That power comes from the people and that people retain the "indubitable, inalienable, and indefeasible right to reform, alter, or abolish" government should it not serve their collective purposes were natural additions in the midst of revolutionary fervor. These rights, established as constitutional in nature by inclusion in the Virginia declaration, hark back to Lockean natural-rights philosophy, which relies heavily on popular consent for the validity of civil government. The rights declaration also abolished inherited offices, separated the legislative and executive powers from the judiciary powers, promised free and frequent elections, and urged that laws not be suspended without legislative consent. Because these provisions were part of a bill of rights, it is evident that republican government had become an essential element in the preservation of civil liberties.

Other provisions are more recognizable as forerunners of the federal Bill of Rights. First among these was a provision that

> in all capital or criminal prosecutions a man hath a right to demand the cause and nature of his accusation, to be confronted with the accusers and witnesses, to call for evidence in his favor, and to a speedy trial by an impartial jury of twelve men of his vicinage, without whose unanimous consent he cannot be found guilty; nor can he be compelled to give evidence against himself; that no man be deprived of his liberty, except by the law of the land or the judgment of his peers.

These familiar guarantees found later in the Fifth and Sixth Amendments to the U.S. Constitution could not be claimed as natural rights, but were statutory and common-law developments deemed preservative of those rights. The Virginia declaration followed these provisions with two more articles that fall within the criminal justice arena. One, apparently lifted from the English Bill of Rights of 1689 and repeated word for word in the Eighth Amendment, stated that "excessive bail ought not be required, nor excessive fines imposed, nor cruel and unusual punishment inflicted." The next, analog to the Fourth Amendment, declared that the English practice of general warrants was "grievous and oppressive, and ought not to be granted." Civil Justice, as in the Seventh Amendment, was also addressed by declaring that jury trials in matters concerning property "ought to be held sacred."

Concerned that those in power might be led down the path of despotism and make use of the army against the people, article 13 stated

> [t]hat a well-regulated militia, composed of the body of the people, trained to arms, is the proper, natural, and safe defence of a free State; that standing armies, in time of peace, should be avoided, as dangerous to liberty; and that in all cases the military should be under strict subordination to, and governed by, the civil power.

The right to bear arms, considered fundamental enough to be included as the Second Amendment to the U.S. Constitution, was viewed as a necessary protection against despotism that fit naturally with a prohibition on peacetime armies and a reliance on civilian control of the military. In the subsequent two centuries, much has changed about our attitudes toward the availability of arms and the existence of a standing military, though perhaps not as much as might generally be believed. An oft-told anecdote, probably apocryphal, involves the issue of a standing army, as it was debated by the Constitutional Convention. On the floor was a motion to limit the army to five thousand soldiers. George Washington, as convention president, could not speak to the issue, but is said to have whispered to a delegate that the motion ought to be amended to ensure, as well, that "no foreign army should invade the United States at any time with more than three thousand troops." The motion obviously failed, but suggests, even if untrue, the pragmatic concerns that tempered American constitutional idealism.

Two other provisions of the Virginia declaration involved freedom of the press and freedom of religion. The first constitutional grounding for a free press was heralded by article 12, which called it "one of the great bulwarks of liberty" that only "despotic governments" attempt to restrain. The declaration also promised "the free exercise of religion, according to the dictates of conscience." Despite the delegates' liberal attitude in calling upon citizens to practice tolerance of other religions, however, they put a religious tinge to their request by stating that it is a "mutual duty of all to practise Christian forbearance, love, and charity towards each other." The conflict between true tolerance and defining that tolerance in Christian terms never occurred to them and remains a continuing challenge in a society that embraces Judeo-Christian norms.

The Virginia constitutional effort was followed by one in Pennsylvania. The convention called by Pennsylvania was chaired by Benjamin Franklin but mostly populated by young radicals whose number included Thomas Paine. John Adams later noted that Pennsylvania's rights charter, passed on August 16, 1776, was "taken almost verbatim" from Virginia's. As did Virginia's, it began with a statement about people's natural rights. Still, Pennsylvania included more liberal protection of religious liberty, gave the people extraordinary power over "internal police," and guaranteed criminal defendants a right to be represented by counsel. Pennsylvania also expanded the right to free expression beyond

State Constitutions Foreshadow the Federal Document

Virginia was one of the first states to draft a bill of rights and constitution after dissolving ties with the British. A close comparison of this document with the Bill of Rights of the U.S. Constitution, enacted almost fifteen years later, highlights interesting similarities.

1. That all men are by nature equally free and independent, and have certain inherent rights, of which, when they enter into a state of society, they cannot by any compact deprive or divest their posterity; namely, the enjoyment of life and liberty, with the means of acquiring and possessing property, and pursuing and obtaining happiness and safety.

2. That all power is vested in, and consequently derived from, the people; that magistrates are their trustees and servants, and at all times amenable to them.

3. That government is, or ought to be instituted for the common benefit, protection, and security of the people, nation, or community; of all the various modes and forms of government, that is best which is capable of producing the greatest degree of happiness and safety, and is most effectually secured against the danger of maladministration; and that when any government shall be found inadequate or contrary to these purposes, a majority of the community hath an indubitable, unalienable and indefeasible right to reform, alter or abolish it, in such manner as shall be judged most conducive to the public weal.

4. That no man, or set of men, are entitled to exclusive or separate emoluments or privileges from the community, but in consideration of publick services; which, not being descendible,

one belonging to the press. Its declaration included a right to free speech and rights of assembly and petition.

Other State Constitutions

Maryland's offering, sounding much like English statutory law, chimed in with rights against ex post facto laws, bills of attainder, poll taxes, and monopolies, but other state consti-

---

neither ought the offices of magistrate, legislator or judge to be hereditary. . . .

12. That the freedom of the press is one of the great bulwarks of liberty, and can never be restrained but by despotick governments.

13. That a well-regulated militia, composed of the body of the people trained to arms, is the proper, natural and safe defence of a free state; that standing armies in time of peace should be avoided as dangerous to liberty; and that in all cases the military should be under strict subordination to, and governed by, the civil power.

14. That the people have a right to uniform government; and, therefore, that no government separate from, or independent of the government of Virginia, ought to be erected or established within the limits thereof.

15. That no free government, or the blessings of liberty, can be preserved to any people, but by a firm adherence to justice, moderation, temperance, frugality and virtue, and by frequent recurrence to fundamental principles.

16. That religion, or the duty which we owe to our Creator, and the manner of discharging it, can be directed only by reason and conviction, not by force or violence; and therefore all men are equally entitled to the free exercise of religion, according to the dictates of conscience; and that it is the mutual duty of all to practise Christian forbearance, love, and charity towards each other.

Morison, Samuel Eliot, ed. *Sources and documents illustrating the American Revolution, 1764–1788 and the Formation of the Federal Constitution.* London: Oxford University Press, 1929.

tutions generally did not add notably to the existing array of rights. However, the federal Constitution's framers could have benefited from a closer examination of Massachusetts's brief constitutional history. It provided forewarning that a constitution without a bill of rights might not pass public muster. A proposed Massachusetts Constitution was rejected by the people of the Bay State in 1778 by a five-to-one margin for failing to "describe the Natural Rights of Man." A convention was called to begin the process anew in 1779, and primary responsibility for the drafting process fell to John Adams, who described his new trade as that of "Constitution monger."

It has frequently been recognized that the early state constitutions "serve as the context of the U.S. Constitution; the rights that eventually appeared in the Bill of Rights appeared first in the state declarations of rights." Among the rights that are familiar in the federal Bill of Rights and were also found in predecessor state constitutions are the right to religious freedom, the right to freedom of speech and of the press, rights of assembly and petition, the right to bear arms, rights against the quartering of soldiers, rights against unreasonable search and seizure, the right to due process, rights of criminal procedure, a right to trial by jury, and rights against excessive bail, fines, and punishments.

These provisions were not always stated in language as broad as that adopted in the federal Constitution. For example, some of the guarantees of religious freedom were followed by provisions that specifically recognized a need for public financial support of religion because of its importance to society or that limited the rights that should be observed to followers of Christian religions. The kind of recognition and public support implied by those provisions would not withstand federal constitutional scrutiny under today's standards, for they run counter to the purposes and modern interpretation of the Establishment Clause.

Other state bill of rights provisions confirmed the ideas of popular sovereignty and natural rights. Additional provisions finding no corollary in their federal counterpart include a guarantee of free elections, a right to travel from state to state, recognition of conscientious objectors' rights, prohibitions against a standing army, a prohibition against the suspension of laws, and an admonition for a frequent return to fundamental principles.

The constitution drafting and the experimentation with rights that occurred in the first states provided significant background for the attempts to define rights on a federal basis. The attempt to reduce those rights to a constitutional writing gave them their fundamental importance. Without the state experiments and the state experiences, a federal bill of rights would not have had the same popular appeal and may never have been written.

Chapter 4

Effects of the Revolution: What Came After?

Turning|Points
IN WORLD HISTORY

The American Revolution Did Not Bring Freedom for Blacks

Donald R. Wright

Donald R. Wright presents a minority viewpoint of the Revolutionary War in his work, *African Americans in the Colonial Era: From African Origins Through the Revolution.* In this excerpt from the book, Wright argues that though many northern blacks were freed after the war under the influence of Enlightenment principles, southern slave-holders were unwilling to dismantle the institution of slavery.

The American Revolution was full of contradictions for African Americans. The clearest contradiction involved slavery and the ideology the Founding Fathers used to justify breaking with England. A third of the men who signed the document declaring their right to independent nationhood on the self-evident truth that all men are created equal owned other humans. In addition, the nation these men would create—the one that would secure the blessings of liberty to themselves and their posterity—was one whose social and economic fabric was woven with the thread of black slavery, whose population included half a million African American slaves, and whose wealthiest southerners would not consider joining a union of states without a clear recognition of their right to own others. . . .

Yet most important for blacks in America over the long term, and probably most ironic, the Revolution brought a broadening and strengthening of the hierarchal order to American race relations. Although most English colonists held strong feelings about race before the Revolution, they did not need to use race so centrally to justify enslaving other human beings. Once Revolutionary theory made all persons free and equal with God-given inalienable rights, many who spoke the new ideals had cause to further entrench their racist feelings. They could rationalize slavery only by recognizing African Americans as a lower order, short on morals, long on muscle, quick to pilfer, slow to move, and hard to work. They could remain above the new and rapidly growing body of free blacks they despised only by using the same rationale. This affected all African Americans and laid the foundation for a stronger and more pervasive racist ideology that would plague the country from the time the Revolution had run its course until the present day.

Westerners had long been in conflict over the existence of slavery in their society. Within the eighteenth-century body of thought we know of as the Enlightenment, strong intellectual forces emerged that worked against chattel slavery. Based initially on religious principles, and then bolstered by philanthropic tendencies accompanying the early growth of capitalism, antislavery sentiment arose in continental Europe and spread to England. By the time of the American Revolution, regardless of what else was going on, Western intellectuals and philosophers were reading and thinking and acting in a world that was debating slavery. . . .

Enlightenment Ideals and Slavery

Many of the men who provided the ideology of the American Revolution considered themselves scions of the Enlightenment. Their faith in Man's limitless creative intelligence and rational, benevolent behavior brought them to apply their minds to creating a new order. No more oppression from religious zealots or tyrannous monarchs, no more misery or deprivation for the people in their society. The new order would provide persons of all classes the freedom to seek happiness and to unleash their talents on their natural circumstances for the benefit of all. The result would be what the rational, benevolent Creator intended.

Of course, it was an ideology into which slavery did not fit, and the American patriots knew it. Like despotism, slavery was a vestige of the Old World, a violation of rights. By being born human, people had rights to freedom, to gain from their work, to improve their lives as they wished. Skin color was not supposed to matter. . . .

In spite of the lofty ideals, the Revolution failed to eradicate slavery from the nation that replaced British rule over the North American mainland. But in raising the issues of freedom and human dignity the Revolution brought change of different shape and order to all parts of American society. For blacks in the northern states and for growing numbers in the Upper South this change meant becoming free persons. For those in the Lower South it meant greater personal independence, but within a slave system that was growing and becoming more deeply entrenched. And the arguments for freedom and the growing presence of free blacks led toward a hardening of racial lines and movement toward a system in which all African Americans, slave or free, would be regarded as members of a despised lower caste. . . .

New African American Society

Up and down the Atlantic Coast and inland toward the newly opening backcountry, the Revolution altered the lives of African Americans. North of Maryland, blacks experienced a gradual expansion of freedoms as slavery there died its slow death. In South Carolina and Georgia, slaves achieved greater independence, but it was independence within a slave system that was growing rapidly and becoming even more entrenched in white society. Blacks in the Chesapeake enjoyed greater freedom, too, with the rapid appearance and growth of the free black population and with more liberties in slavery, but this occurred against a backdrop of growing commitment to slavery through the southern parts of the region. And the geographical parameters of black life in bondage were spreading through the period, for out on the Virginia and Carolina frontiers a new slave society was forming, with implications for further expansion of the institution. . . .

The transition from servitude to freedom in the North was surprisingly difficult. The timing of abolition, which varied by decades among the northern states, affected how slaves made the transition. So did regional demographic patterns, economic conditions, and white attitudes. . . .

Even for those who remained in or around the master's residence, the end of slavery brought African Americans a clear sense of being different people, no longer bound by the personalities or rules of their masters. Studies of slave naming patterns in northern states show how slaves broke with their past almost immediately upon becoming free by ceasing to use the old, derisive first names their masters had given them—

A Petition for Freedom

The sentiments of the Declaration of Independence called out to many people who felt it was written specifically for them. In this excerpt from the New Hampshire legislature in 1779, a group of slaves petitioned to be considered free, and used convincing arguments to make their case. The state House of Representatives listened to the case but determined that the state was not ready for this change.

Permit again your humble slaves to lay before this honorable assembly some of those grievances which they daily experience and feel. Though fortune hath dealt out our portion with rugged hand, yet hath she smiled in the disposal of our persons to those who claim us as their property; of them we do not complain, but from what authority they assume the power to dispose of our lives, freedom and property, we would wish to know. Is it from the sacred volume of Christianity? There we believe it is not to be found; but here hath the cruel hand of slavery made us incompetent judges, hence knowledge is hid from our minds. Is it from the volumes of the laws? Of these also slaves cannot be judges, but those we are told are founded on reason and justice; it cannot be found there. Is it from the volumes of nature? No, here we can read with others, of this knowledge, slavery cannot wholly deprive us; here we know that we ought to be free agents; here we feel the dignity of human nature; here we feel the passions and desires of men, though checked by the rod of slavery; here we feel a just equality; here we know that the God of nature made us free. Is their

the classical Pompey or Caesar, the African day names of Cuffee or Quash, or such place names as York or Jamaica. They moved away also from the surnames of their masters. The names they chose, however, with many biblical first names and more English first and last names, suggest how far acculturation had come for African Americans in the North.

Many blacks in rural areas found seasonal wage labor on small farms near where they lived, but many also moved toward the greater opportunities offered in the northern coastal

---

authority assumed from custom? If so let that custom be abolished, which is not founded in nature, reason nor religion. Should the humanity and benevolence of this honorable assembly restore us that state of liberty of which we have been so long deprived, we conceive that those who are our present masters will not be sufferers by our liberation, as we have most of us spent our whole strength and the prime of our lives in their service; and as freedom inspires a noble confidence and gives the mind an emulation to vie in the noblest efforts of enterprise, and as justice and humanity are the result of your deliberations, we fondly hope that the eye of pity and the heart of justice may commiserate our situation, and put us upon the equality of freemen, and give us an opportunity of evincing to the world our love of freedom by exerting ourselves in her cause, in opposing the efforts of tyranny and oppression over the country in which we ourselves have been so long injuriously enslaved.

Therefore, Your humble slaves most devoutly pray for the sake of injured liberty, for the sake of justice, humanity and the rights of mankind, for the honor of religion and by all that is dear, that your honors would graciously interpose in our behalf, and enact such laws and regulations, as you in your wisdom think proper, whereby we may regain our liberty and be ranked in the class of free agents, and that the name of slave may not more be heard in a land gloriously contending for the sweets of freedom. And your humble slaves as in duty bound will ever pray.

Kutler, Stanley I. *Looking for America: The People's History*. Vol. 1: New York: W.W. Norton and Company, 1979.

cities. African American populations of Boston, New York, and Philadelphia soared with the ending of the war. New York's population of free blacks lagged behind the others because of the continuing existence of a large slave population. Philadelphia attracted newly freed blacks and runaways from Maryland and Virginia to the extent that between 1780 and 1800, while the city's white population was doubling, its African American population was increasing sixfold.

Part of the lure of northern cities was economic opportunity. If the urban setting offered little room or advancement, it still held the possibility of sustaining oneself on a low level. More African American women moved to the city than men because jobs for domestics were always plentiful. Most men worked as day laborers, especially in the maritime industry, but urban blacks held positions as artisans and shopkeepers in about the same numbers as when slavery existed there.

The city also offered free blacks the advantage of living with others of their culture. Blacks living in small numbers in the northern countryside were isolated and thus targets for white hostility, which rose with the ending of slavery. But in the city, African Americans in good numbers lived near one another and soon black community institutions existed that provided them security. It was in the city that men and women could more easily find marriage partners and begin families; it was there they could join in worship, combine resources to educate their young, and come together for camaraderie and mutual support.

Freedom was surprisingly disruptive and hard on African American families. By 1770 most of black society in America had its basis in the family. Becoming free and moving away from the master's household disturbed the family's stability. In addition to normal problems associated with poverty, especially husbands and wives being too poor to live together, black families often experienced the unsettling circumstances of moving and resettling. It would take time to create stable family life in a new setting. Once extricated from white residences but not yet able to form their own nuclear households, poor blacks often combined with relatives or friends to establish separate residences. Taking in boarders helped pay expenses. Transition to a pattern of two-parent households took about a generation from abolition. Yet far from being the unstable, matrilocal institution that social scientists long portrayed, the postabolition African American family in the North became stable and autonomous soon after it appeared. Both parents lived at home and played important roles in the maintenance of the household.

In rural areas black residence patterns remained separate and varied, but in northern cities one could see by the 1780s the beginnings of a pattern of residential clustering and the formation of small but integral neighborhoods. Separate black churches appeared, initially as refuges from discrimination in white churches and as places where blacks could worship in the emotional fashion they preferred. Churches provided burial grounds, centers for common activities, and seedbeds for formation of benevolent and fraternal organizations. Congregations pooled their resources and started "African" schools for training their young. . . .

Slavery Strengthens in the South

If the Revolution first brought questioning and then the demise of slavery in the North, it generally failed to cause whites in the country's southern extreme to reflect seriously on the rectitude of slave society. In fact, slavery in South Carolina and Georgia began a period of entrenchment and expansion just as the institution began to die in the northern states. The result by the end of the Revolutionary era would be the existence of a more powerful and viable southern institution, with prominent whites sure of slavery's necessity and, therefore, adamant about their right to own and forcibly work other humans. For the slaves, ironically, the same period brought still greater autonomy and, with a new wave of importation of Africans, a reinvigoration of the subculture that was more "African" than any other on the mainland. . . .

By war's end, countless African Americans in South Carolina had died, disappeared, or gained their freedom. . . . The colony's black population was reduced by about one-quarter—twenty-five thousand men and women. More Georgia slaves actually escaped through the period, seven thousand to British lines and untold numbers to Spanish lands or Indian territory to the south and west.

The war had long-term effects for the blacks who remained. British occupation and the chaos in the countryside left a void in control. South Carolina slaves did not run away in the numbers owners feared because of continual, more careful patrolling and because both sides in the war discouraged runaways. South Carolina's white leaders "received with horror" a Continental congress proposal in 1779 to recruit slave soldiers, and British forces were hardly armies of liberation. Without resources to handle large numbers of dependents, and never having much desire to liberate enslaved African Americans anyway (since many loyalists were slave owners), the British army rationalized that the slaves were "ungovernable" and saw to it that they stayed put.

Out on the plantation, sometimes left alone for weeks or months at a time, African Americans carved out new, more liberal bounds for their activities. Black slave drivers, already powerful with the frequent absence of owners, became more involved in planning and management. Their authority reached new levels. Other slaves took on greater responsibilities, accumulated more property, and participated more in interplantation commerce and regional trade. Once the English left and the planters returned, it was practically impossible to return to the old, more restrictive ways of low-country plantation life. . . .

The greater independence of all South Carolina and Georgia blacks allowed them to strengthen family ties and broaden their already strong, hybrid subculture. After the Revolution, more African American men and women on plantations were able to live with their families, which now extended over several generations, and owners showed more respect for the family units of their slaves. African American culture remained divided as before the Revolution, with urban slaves more acculturated and rural blacks clinging to African customs. The reinstitution of the slave trade after the war's end brought a final influx of African elements into low-country black culture and insured that it would continue to have strong African influences. . . .

Yet the end of the Revolutionary years saw low-country landowners believing more strongly than ever in the efficacy of the slave system and more willing and able to perpetuate that system. In the low country the idea that acquiring slaves was the way to prosperity flourished; nowhere in the new country was it more current. Soon after the end of hostilities, the economy of the low country boomed. Georgia first and then South Carolina reopened the Atlantic trade and rapidly imported enough Africans to replace losses from the war. They continued to import large numbers of Africans so that whites could move to the backcountry with their laborers. The power and wealth of southern landowners began increasing as the system of slave labor expanded to include the growing of new crops. The indigo market disappeared with the loss of the English market in the war years, but planters began growing a new crop, cotton, and that started spreading slowly inland after 1790. By 1800 slavery in the low country had new life. South Carolina and Georgia planters should be in good positions to take advantage of opportunities the expanding economy would offer them.

Slavery in the Chesapeake

In Virginia and Maryland the Revolution brought even greater dislocation and change. Blacks and whites appeared on the move everywhere and to some the movement seemed to be turning society about. In Virginia there was westward movement toward the Blue Ridge. Some slave owners took their bondsmen out of reach of the fighting; others merely saw advantage in establishing upland farms on fertile new lands. Those who stayed recognized the heavily creole slave population would grow rapidly through natural increase. Slaves and land were available. As the market for tobacco fell with the war, Chesapeake planters turned to mixed farming. Although tidewater soils had lost fertility over the generations of tobacco growing, planters relied on increasing numbers of black workers to squeeze profits from the land.

Farmers in the Upper Chesapeake did not have the outlet of a western frontier. Planters in Maryland already had turned to producing cereal, which thrived on small farms with free labor, so slavery did not grow and expand as in the central and southern parts of Virginia. Slave prices fell in Maryland, and although the numbers of persons in bondage grew in the Upper Chesapeake for two decades after the war, the Revolution marked the beginning of the splitting of Chesapeake slave society. In Maryland and northernmost Virginia slavery would be less important for the economy and there would be a movement toward greater freedom. In the central and southern Virginia Piedmont and Tidewater the trend would be in the opposite direction. Slavery became more entrenched, the number of white slaveholders increased, and the African American population grew rapidly by natural increase as the nineteenth century approached.

Free blacks in the Chesapeake went through changes similar to those in the North. They found jobs, took new residences, changed names, reconstructed families or made new ones, and slowly developed the community institutions—schools, churches, benevolent societies—that helped ease the social transition, prepared people for life's problems, and provided individuals a communal identity. . . .

Conclusions

By the end of the Revolution, ironic circumstances appeared in African American society. On the one hand there was the new, clear division between free blacks and those enslaved that was similar in many ways to the old split between Africans and creoles. But on the other was the first indication of broad unity across the breadth of all African American society. As always, regional variants of black society continued to evolve in their own fashion, and there remained obvious differences in black ways of life. No doubt it was difficult to recognize social commonalities between African Americans living in Philadelphia, for example, and Gullah slaves on low-country plantations. Also, the waning social and cultural split between Africans and slaves born in America lingered in the South Carolina and Georgia backcountry.

But beyond these divisions was a hint of the emergence of the broad African American cultural unity that would eventually prevail. Hardening racial attitudes of whites and their growing inclinations to separate and treat in discriminating fashion everyone of African descent, regardless of servile status, brought African Americans to recognize what they had in common. In addition to their African heritage and such unifying manifestations of culture as religious practice, close kinship ties, and general folkways, free blacks were not so long out of slavery and not welcome enough in white society to lose contact and identity with their cultural counterparts in bondage. As a result, as African American society continued to evolve—indeed, as free blacks in the North and Upper South proceeded to grasp what advantages they could find while southern blacks were becoming involved in a slave system of expanding scope and importance—it became more evident that their lots were cast together. By 1800, African Americans were part of a single American society. Over the long run of the nineteenth century, what befell one group would come to affect the other. . . .

Before the eighteenth century was over a clear tendency to separate the races was becoming evident. This was neither necessary nor possible on plantations and smaller farms, but in cities throughout the country whites moved to exclude all African Americans, free or slave, from social activities where whites were involved. In public facilities African Americans got separate, inferior accommodations. White churches either proscribed blacks or treated them as second-class members. Restaurants and taverns moved blacks to separate sections; clubs, fraternal organizations, and trade unions simply refused to admit them to membership. African Americans were not welcome in white schools or, in many cases, in white cemeteries. The issue was not slavery. It was race.

Such patterns of segregation seldom needed to be written into law. They entered into custom and became society's norms. These customs spread out of the South and across the free states through the first half of the nineteenth century. From the end of the colonial era, racist ideas and practices of separation would be part of American patterns of thought and modes of behavior for two more centuries of African American life.

The Class System Remains

Dan Lacy

Dan Lacy, noted scholar of the American Revolution, served as the assistant national archivist of the United States. Lacy examines the aftermath of the American Revolution, especially who would be chosen to lead the country and who would be able to vote. After a revolution and in a nation based on liberty and equality, early American politics did not reflect these same tenets.

When the rebels declared that all men are created equal they were trying to find a general argument to support a very specific case: that Americans were created equal to Englishmen and hence equally entitled to govern themselves. But the argument outran its goal. If Americans were created equal to Englishmen, were they not created equal to each other? If it was no longer tolerable that Britons through their representatives in Parliament should have an unearned, inherited privilege to tax the property of unrepresented Americans, was it tolerable that disfranchised Americans should be taxed by the legislatures of their own states, in which they were equally unrepresented? If all men are equal, was it just that members of a dominant faith have advantage over those of other sects or that a rich man should have greater political rights than a poor man? If all men are created equal, what justification could be found to divide them into freemen and slaves and to allow men of one group to buy and sell those of the other?

Though the American colonies in pre-Revolutionary days were freer from structured privilege than any other commonwealths in the world, inequalities nevertheless existed; and for decades before the Revolution there had been strug-

Excerpted from Dan Lacy, *The Meaning of the American Revolution*. (New York: New American Library, 1964). Reprinted by permission of the author.

gles to reduce or to perpetuate them. The conflicts of low countryman and frontiersman, of rich man and poor, of the established churches and the dissenters, had gone on side by side with the controversies between colonial assemblies and royal governors. These two sets of conflicts sometimes coincided, sometimes cut across each other. Sometimes the same men were fighting both for equality within the British empire and for equality at home, like the Whig leaders in New York or Massachusetts. More often, perhaps, the American leaders were members of oligarchies within their own colonies who sought to win from the distant British a greater power for those local oligarchies and at the same time to preserve their power from dilution at home. In North Carolina, for example, the Revolutionary leaders were the same men who half a dozen years before had supported the royal governor in suppressing the Regulator movement among the disadvantaged frontiersmen; and the Regulators of 1771 for the most part either supported the Crown or were indifferent when the Revolution itself came. . . .

Voting and Property

The manifestations of inequality and Privilege against which the more egalitarian rebels struggled were numerous. One of them was a universal limitation of suffrage to persons of some property. In most colonies this limitation followed the British precedent of confining the votes to those holding a freehold in property worth forty shillings a year or more in rent. In view of the wide dispersion of real property and the ease with which land could be acquired, this limitation was not so restrictive as in Great Britain, where it confined the suffrage to a tiny minority. But even in America the exclusion of the landless—the farm laborer, the footloose itinerant, the urban workman—narrowed the franchise to a point where the number of voters was rarely so much as ten percent of the free adult male population. The total exclusion from the vote of women and slaves was a matter of course.

Even among those who could vote there was a further inequality in terms of representation. In almost every colony the older settlements along the coast, usually dominated by the wealthier and more conservative elements, hung on to an unequal voice in the legislature. Sometimes, as in North Carolina and Pennsylvania, this was achieved by giving the older counties more delegates than the new, regardless of population. In other colonies there was a refusal to create new frontier counties, leaving the very large populations of enormous western counties with the same representation as the tiny counties of the east. This imbalance reached perhaps its extreme form in South Carolina, where the upland settlements were not organized into counties at all and hence went entirely unrepresented.

Property qualifications were even more rigid with respect to officeholding, and the assemblies were in consequence likely to be made up of men of very substantial means. The large-propertied and professional classes were given a further privilege through their dominance of the appointive or indirectly elected governors' councils, which shared legislative power with the elective assemblies.

Local Government by the Privileged

Except for the town meetings of New England—which were even more democratic than the relatively democratic assemblies of those colonies—local government was a stronghold of privilege. County government in most of the other colonies, as in England, was in the hands of a Court of Pleas and Quarter Sessions, which served as a trial court as well as the governing body of the county. It was made up of justices of the peace who individually exercised a large judicial and administrative power within their respective neighborhoods. Though officially elected by the assembly or appointed by the governor, the county court was likely to be a self-perpetuating body in practice, immune from popular control, and representing the large-property interests of the county. Insofar as the cities outside New England had been incorporated, their governments were likely to be legally, as well as practically, self-perpetuating "close corporations" in which a named group of burgesses made up the corporation and had power to fill vacancies in their number, or in which the burgesses were elected by a very restricted suffrage. City governments outside New England were likely to represent the larger merchants in the same way that county governments represented the larger landowners.

The opportunity to acquire land easily and cheaply had been the principal dynamic force driving toward equality in the colonies. Individual ownership of small farms was in itself an assurance of relative equality in an overwhelmingly agricultural society. But the influence of cheap land extended further. It strengthened the position of artisans and laborers, who could take up land as an alternative to continuing an oppressive or unrewarding employment. So long as land was easily come by, the limitation of the suffrage to property owners was not so harsh a restriction. To the extent that the opportunity to own land was freely and equally available, freedom and equality flowed out to all other aspects of colonial life. But in the years before the Revolution this opportunity was narrowing. Because of the primitive state of roads, only lands near water transportation were valuable for anything but subsistence farming, and most such lands had passed into private hands by the mid-eighteenth century. The remaining ungranted lands were, as Curtis Nettels has pointed out, vested in the Crown and in five proprietors: two Penn brothers, Lord Baltimore, Lord Fairfax, and Lord Granville, who owned lands in Pennsylvania, Maryland, Virginia, and North Carolina and Tennessee, respectively. All of these proprietors were interested in exploiting their property for a maximum return under quasi-feudal tenures, which normally meant large grants to wealthy purchasers. The line of settlement was pressing against the mountains, and the Crown in 1763, by drawing its Proclamation Line along the crest of the Appalachians, closed off to legal settlement the great reservoir of fertile land in the West. Negotiations were under way in the following decade, with several wealthy syndicates seeking to monopolize princely grants in the Ohio and Indiana areas. In 1774 the Quebec Act placed lands west of the mountains and north of the Ohio under the French feudal forms of land tenure used in Quebec. A pattern of restrictive and oligopolistic land ownership seemed about to replace the relative equality of the earlier days.

Legal patterns in some of the colonies further reinforced this trend. In New York the Dutch practice of granting vast patroonships with the characteristics of feudal estates was continued by the English, with the result that most of the valuable land in that province was vested in a few families like the Philipses, the Van Rensselaers, the Van Cortlandts, the Schuylers, and the Livingstons. Royal governors in other colonies, like New Hampshire and Georgia, were enabled to endow themselves with vast estates. Of special importance in the Southern colonies were the British practices of primogeniture and entail. Primogeniture assured the inheritance of landed estates by the eldest son in the absence of a specific will to the contrary. Entail was a legal procedure under which an owner could assure that his estate would pass down the male line of his heirs intact from generation to generation without being sold or divided. Both practices encouraged the formation and perpetuation of great landed properties after the British and European form.

Other Restrictions on Voting

Though a diversity of sects and the high degree of lay control of most of them made the churches much less an instrument of privilege in America than in Europe, Congregationalists in New England and Anglicans in the South did enjoy special privileges. Their clergy and churches were supported by the income from church lands granted by the colony and by taxes levied on all residents except for active members of certain recognized dissenting sects. Religious qualifications for officeholding in many colonies gave a further advantage to the adherents of the traditional faiths. The establishment of the Congregational Church in New England and the Anglican Church in the Southern colonies had a political and economic as well as a religious significance in that these were the churches of the older, well-established, prosperous settlers of the coastal area. The less well-to-do frontiersmen, already suffering from underrepresentation and inability to acquire fertile and well-situated land, and frequently deprived of the vote, suffered another handicap from the inferior status of their Presbyterian, Baptist, and German churches.

A further barrier to equality existed in the character of the educational system. Except in parts of New England, the school system was entirely private, and a child's education depended on the willingness and ability of his parents to pay for it. Moreover, there were few or no schools in the more thinly settled frontier areas, even for the parent who could afford to school his children. Again, the prosperous resident of port towns and the tidewater could pass on to his sons a more privileged opportunity of success than could the poor man or the frontiersman.

The traditions of the common law, as amplified in colonial statutes, had a care for the security of the well-to-do rather than for the suffering of the poor. Only the meager bounty of the parish fund protected the poor from catastrophe, and even this shelter was available only to settled folk, who were rarely those who needed it most. Rigorous sanctions of the law, however, protected the well-to-do in their right to collect debts due them, including the power to imprison a debtor unable to pay. In a day of very poor credit arrangements, without banks or other organized sources of loans, and with a limited and rigid money supply, perhaps most farmers and many small businessmen were dependent at one time or another upon loans from individual men of wealth. These loans were often difficult to repay promptly because of a shortage of hard money in the community generally, crop failures, the loss of ships at sea, or any one of dozens of unpredictable disasters that might befall in an economy far less well cushioned against misfortune than ours. Hard money and rigid collection, enforced by foreclosure and debtors prison, were the security of the well-to-do and the terror of those less fortunate. . . .

Changing Land Policies

Since most of the restrictions on voting and officeholding were expressed in terms of the ownership of real property, their actual significance depended on the distribution of land. Here the consequences of the Revolution were truly revolutionary. The ownership of hundreds of millions of acres passed from the Crown and from various lords to the people of the United States or of the individual states. We have already pointed out that the long policy debate over the Trans-Appalachian West was finally and definitely resolved in favor of its rapid settlement by individual farmers to whom the land would be given cheaply. Gone were all ideas of preserving the area for the Indians or of restricting the flow of settlement to facilitate British control or to continue the dominant position of the Atlantic states. By the ordinances of 1785 and 1787, already described, the Western lands were thrown open on a democratic basis, and with the relatively easy ownership of land would flow a comparably easy access to full political status.

A similar democratization took place within the individual states. In the Southern states and in New York and Pennsylvania there were princely domains taken over from the Crown, or in Pennsylvania the proprietor, and not ceded to the Confederation. All of the states adopted relatively liberal policies in disposing of the possessions. A very large part of the state lands were used as bounties to encourage enlistment in the Revolutionary armies, thus speeding up its dispersion into private hands.

A third process important in democratizing land ownership was the confiscation and resale of loyalist estates. The states generally, by legislative acts early in the war, authorized the seizure of the property of those who remained actively loyal to the Crown. Enormous estates were involved. Many of the royal governors, like Wentworth in New Hampshire and Wright in Georgia, had managed to gain large domains for themselves; and these were, of course, among those confiscated. The largest loyalist estates were in New York, where most of the great landholdings along the Hudson were seized, along with nearly a quarter of a million acres held by Sir John Johnson in the frontier areas of the state. All told, more than two million five hundred thousand acres, including some of the best land in the state, was taken from fifty-nine loyalists who had monopolized these thousands of square miles. Though many of the loyalist lands were bid in by wealthy men who were themselves already large landowners, there can be no doubt that the breakup of these domains markedly changed the economic constitution of such states as New York.

Moreover, the legal structure was itself changed throughout the states to discourage the future creation or maintenance of estates of this size. The new land policies were aimed at granting family-sized holdings rather than the patroonships and quasibaronies of the colonial period. An attack was also made on the laws of primogeniture and entail that helped to hold the great estates together. Virginia abolished entails in 1776, and within a decade all other states had also done away with them or so modified them as to make them meaningless. Primogeniture was more stubbornly supported, but by 1789 it too had been abolished in Georgia, Maryland, New York, North Carolina, and Virginia. In other states, such as most of those in New England, the rights of the eldest son had been confined to a double portion, but this too was abolished in the Revolutionary period. By 1789 primogeniture survived only in Rhode Island and South Carolina, and it was on its way out there.

All told, the changes in the legal structure of land tenure that took place during the Revolution may have been the most significant of all the democratizing trends of the period. . . .

Democracy and Education

The more thoughtful Revolutionary leaders realized that a democratic government could be safely based only on a democratic educational system. To vote intelligently, a citizen must have the minimum of literacy that would enable him to use newspapers and books to form his own opinions. If officeholding were to be truly open to the people, then opportunities for higher education must be open to the abler children of whatever social class.

In the New England states this ideal had been approached. The Calvinist religion, with its emphasis on the responsibility of every man to read and interpret the Bible for himself, had provided a powerful sanction for universal education, which in turn accorded with the democratic organization of society in that region. Moreover, each of the New England colonies had a college, again intended primarily for the production of learned clergymen but serving the lay needs of society as well. The Middle colonies as well boasted a college each—two in New Jersey—and although education was almost entirely in the hands of the churches and private charities, the region was wealthy enough to provide a fairly general access to elementary education. The South, however, lagged far behind. There was no public or regularly organized church or charitable provision for elementary education, and William and Mary was the only college in the entire region. In consequence of these regional differences, literacy was nearly universal in New England, and the son of a plain farmer like John Adams, if his abilities permitted, could readily obtain an excellent classical education. In the South, in contrast, over half the white men, most white women, and substantially all Negroes were illiterate: and a college education was usually reserved for the sons of wealthy planters. This education system—or lack of it—reflected and powerfully reinforced the aristocratic structure of Southern society. The situation in the Middle states lay between these extremes.

As early as 1765 John Adams, speaking of a common school system, had pointed out that "the preservation of the means of knowledge among the lowest ranks is of more importance to the public than all the property of all the rich men in the country." Jefferson emphatically shared this conviction and indeed proposed to the Virginia legislature a scheme by which all children other than those of slaves would receive a tax-supported education through the third grade, that is, through the basic skills of reading, writing, and common arithmetic; the more gifted would receive secondary training, still at public expense; and the ablest of all would receive their education free at a state university. Numbers of other leaders of the time had similar views, and it was a part of the standard beliefs of the time that political and educational quality must go hand in hand.

The Revolutionary epoch saw little done to achieve these ends. The war years themselves were, in fact, almost disastrous for education. The disorders of war and the preoccupation with the war effort closed hundreds of schools. The small endowments of the nine colleges that existed at the beginning of the war were dissipated by inflation, the buildings of several were occupied by British and American troops, and faculty and students were drawn into the war. Nevertheless, the devotion to educational ideals in the period was not wholly wasted; and if little was accomplished, much was planned and a good deal was begun.

John Adams, in his *Thoughts on Government*, written in 1776 as a guide to the making of new constitutions for the soon-to-be states, renewed his earlier appeals for public education. "Laws for the liberal education of youth, especially of the lower class of people, are so extremely wise and useful that to a humane and generous mind no expense for this purpose would be thought extravagant." His words found a definite, if modest response. New Hampshire (in its second constitution), Massachusetts, Pennsylvania, North Carolina, and Georgia in their new constitutions all made provisions of one kind or another for publicly supported education, as did Vermont on its subsequent admission to the Union. Connecticut and Rhode Island continued their colonial provisions for town-supported schools along with their colonial charters. In New York, though the constitution was silent on education, immediately after the end of hostilities Governor Clinton made an eloquent appeal to the legislature for a statewide educational program. As he put it in 1782, ". . . it is the peculiar duty of the government of a free state where the highest employments are open to citizens of every rank to endeavor by the establishment of schools and seminars to diffuse that degree of literature which is necessary to the establishment of public trusts." His appeal led to the passage of acts in 1784, 1785, and 1787 that created a "University of the State of New York," responsible for all education in the state, and a Board of Regents to govern it, and that set aside certain public lands for the support of education. Delaware's legislature made a more modest commitment to public schools.

In 1785 Georgia passed legislation somewhat similar to New York's, and both that state and North Carolina made provision for state universities. Though these institutions were not in fact to open until 1795 in the case of North Carolina and 1801 in the case of Georgia, they were the first two state universities in the country.

Poverty was to prevent any very realistic effort to carry out these ambitious projects, and a genuine system of public schools providing universal primary education would have to await the mid-nineteenth century. But by 1789 most of the states by one means or another had made a commitment to the ideal of free, tax-supported, education as an essential basis of democracy. The idea became part of the foundation of the American political philosophy.

Meanwhile private efforts were doing a good deal to enlarge educational opportunity. Dozens of "academies" were opened in the postwar decade, of which the most notable were those endowed by the Phillips family at Andover, Massachusetts, and Exeter, New Hampshire. Numerous colleges were also started, including Dickinson and Franklin colleges in Pennsylvania; the forerunner of Union College in New York; Washington, Saint John's, Cokesbury, and Georgetown in Maryland; and Hampden-Sydney in Virginia. In the twenty years after Yorktown, the number of colleges in the United States more than doubled.

There was also a more serious effort to engage the new academies and colleges more directly with the problems of democratic citizenship. Courses in science were enlarged, and new ones introduced in modern languages, political science, and economics.

The long relation between democracy and education in America had barely begun, but it had begun.

The Constitutional Convention: The Writing of the Constitution

Catherine Drinker Bowen

Catherine Drinker Bowen, the author of several books about American Revolutionary history including *John Adams and the American Revolution*, here discusses the apprehension that the leaders of the new United States felt toward rewriting their constitution. The transition from the Articles of Confederation to the United States Constitution was not easy, as the Articles had served the nation well during the war. But for the continued existence of the United States, the men of the Revolution needed to create a governmental structure that would carry the nation to this day.

Over Philadelphia the air lay hot and humid; old people said it was the worst summer since 1750. A diarist noted that cooling thunderstorms were not so frequent or violent as formerly. Perhaps the new "installic rods" everywhere fixed on the houses might have robbed the clouds of their electric fluid. French visitors wrote home they could not breathe. "At each inhaling of air, one worries about the next one. The slightest movement is painful."

In the Pennsylvania State House, which we call Independence Hall, some fifty-five delegates, named by the legislatures of twelve states (Rhode Island balked, refusing attendance), met in convention, and during the summer of hard work and high feeling wrote out a plan of government which they hoped the states would accept, and which they entitled *The Constitution of the United States of America*.

It was May when the Convention met, it would be September before they rose. Here were some of the most notable names in America; among them Washington, Madison, Hamilton, Benjamin Franklin; John Rutledge and the two Pinckneys from South Carolina; the two Morrises—Robert and Gouverneur; John Dickinson of Delaware; George Wythe, George Mason and John Blair of Virginia; Roger Sherman of Connecticut; Rufus King and Elbridge Gerry of Massachusetts. The roster reads like a Fourth of July oration, a patriotic hymn. It was a young gathering. Charles Pinckney was twenty-nine; Alexander Hamilton, thirty. Rufus King was thirty-two, Jonathan Dayton of New Jersey, twenty-six. Gouverneur Morris—he of the suave manners and the wooden leg—was thirty-five. Even that staid and careful legal scholar, James Madison of Virginia, known today as "father of the Constitution," was only thirty-six. Benjamin Franklin's eighty-one years raised the average considerably, but it never went beyond forty-three. Men aged sooner and died earlier in those days. John Adams at thirty-seven, invited to give a speech in Boston, had said he was "too old to make declamations."

Richard Henry Lee wrote from Virginia that he was glad to find in the Convention "so many gentlemen of competent years." Yet even the youngest member was politically experienced. Nearly three-fourths had sat in the Continental Congress. Many had been members of their state legislatures and had helped to write their state constitutions in the first years after Independence. Eight had signed the Declaration, seven had been state governors, twenty-one had fought in the Revolutionary War. When Jefferson in Paris read the names he said it was "an assembly of demi-gods."

Even so, the Convention was a chancy thing. Delegates showed themselves nervous, apprehensive, but only to each other. Sessions were secret and very little news leaked out; members wrote guardedly to their friends. Neither to the delegates nor to the country at large was this meeting known as a *constitutional* Convention. How could it be? The title came later. The notion of a new "constitution" would have scared away two-thirds of the members. Newspapers announced a Grand Convention at Philadelphia, or spoke of the "Fœderal

Convention," always with the nice inclusion of the classical diphthong. Within doors and without, men were tentative as to what they were devising and what they wanted devised. Congress, meeting in New York during the previous February, had sanctioned this Philadelphia convention *"for the sole and express purpose of revising the Articles of Confederation."* Congress had said nothing about a new constitution. To the thirteen states the Articles of Confederation were constitution enough; since 1781 they had made shift under its aegis. . . .

Revising the Articles of Confederation

The country was by no means blind to the fact that the Articles of Confederation were inadequate and needed mending. Successive presidents of Congress sent letters to the state legislatures, urging them not only to pay their requisitions but to vote additional powers to Congress. State executives asked their local legislatures to recommend that Congressional powers be strengthened. Yet nothing happened, every effort fell through. Among those who began early to work for reform, three names stand out: Washington, Madison and Hamilton. And of the three, evidence points to Hamilton as the most potent single influence toward calling the Convention of '87, though historians still argue the point and Madison's biographers are at pains to give him the palm. Yet if Madison saw logically what ought to happen and if Hamilton expressed it brilliantly, Washington from the first had felt the situation most deeply; his letters during the war were hot with anger and indignation. His troops lacked shoes, meat, gunpowder, clothing, barracks, medicines. "Our sick naked," he wrote; "our well naked, our unfortunate men in captivity naked." Was Congress then helpless in the face of the army's plight? Express riders went out from camps at Cambridge, Harlem Heights, Morristown, Valley Forge, bearing messages signed by the Commander in Chief: "Morristown, May 27, 1780. It is with infinite pain that I inform Congress that we are reduced again to a situation of extremity for want of meat." Congress, powerless, unsupported by the state assemblies, said stubbornly: "Last war, soldiers supplied their own clothing.". . .

Washington owed his own title to Congress, which had elected him by ballot as General of the Continental Army. (Some called it the Grand American Army.) Civilian control of the military was a cardinal principle of the Revolution. "We don't choose to trust you generals with too much power for too long a time," John Adams told Horatio Gates. It was Congress that had enacted the Rules and Regulations for the Government of the Army. But Washington complained that until and unless these rules were altered the army might as well disband—he could not discipline his men, shoot deserters, or properly punish soldiers who stole horses and hospital stores from the army or who burned and plundered houses near the camps. Among the troops, local attachments were fierce and easily aroused. Washington tried to persuade his New Jersey troops to swear allegiance to the United States. They refused. "New Jersey is our country!" they said stubbornly. In Congress a New Jersey member denounced the General's action as improper. . . .

Alexander Hamilton during the war had acted as Washington's aide-de-camp. It was an extraordinary friendship between the young lawyer, foreign-born, impatient, quick, and his Commander in Chief, infinitely steady, with a slow prescience of his own. Concerning Congress and the states, the two saw eye to eye. Moreover, Hamilton worked on Washington, urging him to a strong stand, frequently drafting the General's public statements toward that end. From headquarters at Liberty Pole, New Jersey, in September of 1780, Hamilton wrote his friend Duane a now famous letter—his first clear exposition of the need for a constitutional convention. Covering seventeen printed pages, the letter is an amazing document from anybody's pen, let alone a man in his early twenties, born outside the continent. It was impossible, wrote Hamilton, to govern through thirteen sovereign states. A want of power in Congress made the government fit neither for war nor for peace. "There is only one remedy—to call a convention of all the states." And the sooner the better, Hamilton said. Moreover, the people should first be prepared "by sensible and popular writings."

For the ensuing seven years, Hamilton never stopped

driving and pushing for a convention. He wrote letters private and public, made speeches, published a series of newspaper articles entitled "The Continentalist"—the title alone betrayed his position. The crying need, Hamilton urged, was for a government suited, not to "the narrow colonial sphere in which we have been accustomed to move." Rather, he wished for "that enlarged kind suited to the government of an independent nation." Although not a member of the New York state legislature, in 1782 he persuaded them to pass a resolution urging a convention. Elected to Congress that same year, Hamilton drafted a similar proposal, but with no success.

The states would not listen. Why go outside of Congress? Rufus King, representative from Massachusetts, declared that Congress was "the proper body to propose alterations." To John Adams, King wrote that Congress could "do all a Convention can, and certainly with more safety to original principles."

Original principles signified Revolutionary principles; the Federal Convention was to find that phrase very useful. And it meant whatever men chose it to mean: to men like Governor Clinton of New York, Judge Bryan of Pennsylvania, Patrick Henry, young James Monroe or Congressman Grayson of Virginia, original principles signified as little government as possible, a federation wherein each state would remain sovereign, with Congress at their disposal. Had not the Articles of Confederation been written with this idea uppermost? It had taken five years, beginning in 1776, to write the Articles, argue and vote on them in Congress, modify them, compromise, and finally persuade the last state to ratify. The Articles were in fact America's first constitution. "The Stile of this Confederacy," said Article I, "shall be 'The United States of America.'" Nothing less than the perils of war would have induced the states to make even this tenuous union at a time when John Adams referred to Massachusetts Bay as "our country," and to the Massachusetts representatives as "our embassy." Danger had proved a strong cement.

Only through the persistence and skilled maneuvering of

a few men did the Federal Convention meet at all. It happened that Maryland and Virginia were engaged in a strenuous quarrel over the navigation of the Potomac River; in the spring of 1785, their respective legislatures sent commissioners to Mount Vernon for a discussion of the subject, bearing on the question of east-west communication in general. Seeing the chance to enlist the cooperation of neighboring states, the commission was enlarged, and met at Annapolis in September of 1786. Madison attended; Hamilton came down from New York.

Before the Annapolis Commission rose it had recommended to Congress (Hamilton wrote the report) that all thirteen states appoint delegates to convene at Philadelphia "on the second of May next, to take into consideration the trade and commerce of the United States."

Commerce was a far-reaching word; it covered a multitude of troubles. The war debt still hung heavy; states found their credit failing and small hope of betterment. Seven states had resorted to paper money. True, the postwar depression was lifting. But prosperity remained a local matter; money printed by Pennsylvania must be kept within Pennsylvania's own borders. State and section showed themselves jealous, preferring to fight each other over boundaries as yet unsettled and to pass tariff laws against each other. New Jersey had her own customs service; New York was a foreign nation and must be kept from encroachment. States were marvelously ingenious at devising mutual retaliations; nine of them retained their own navies. (Virginia had even ratified the peace treaty separately.) The shipping arrangements of Connecticut, Delaware and New Jersey were at the mercy of Pennsylvania, New York and Massachusetts. . . .

The Delegates

Seventy-four delegates were named to the Convention at Philadelphia; in the end fifty-five turned up. Two men of eloquence were absent; the Convention missed them but felt their hand. John Adams was in London, Thomas Jefferson in Paris, arranging treaties of commerce and foreign loans and trying to persuade the powers—France, Holland and the rest—that the infant United States could be trusted to meet obligations and pay her debts. Both men were vitally interested in the Convention; letters went back and forth. Adams's book on constitutions past and present, just off the press, circulated among members, receiving praise or blame according to the reader's view of federalism in general and a bicameral legislature in particular.

Congress, sitting in New York, complained of losing members to the Convention at Philadelphia. Since the war ended it had been difficult enough to obtain a quorum. Members simply stayed home, preferring state interests to the general government. (When the treaty of peace had arrived from Paris in 1783, only seven states were represented—two short of the quorum necessary for ratification.) Letters had to be dispatched, urging attendance. Congress was in bad enough case without its best-qualified men taking coach for Pennsylvania. In April of '87 a motion was actually brought to adjourn and move to Philadelphia. The measure failed, though it irked representatives not to know exactly what was brewing. At the moment, Congress sat upstairs in New York's City Hall, described as "a magnificent pile of buildings in Wall Street—more than twice the width of the State House in Boston, but not so long." New York was only one of many Congressional homes. Since the year 1774 a harried legislature had met in Philadelphia, Baltimore, Lancaster, York, Princeton, Annapolis, Trenton—chased from pillar to post by war or, in one case, by mutinying ill-paid soldiers of the Pennsylvania militia.

On the twenty-ninth of May, William Grayson of Virginia complained that Congress was very thin, and that he had heard the Convention at Philadelphia might sit as long as three months. "What will be the result of their meeting I cannot with any certainty determine, but I hardly think much good can come of it: the people of America don't appear to me to be ripe for any great innovations.". . .

Delegates drifted slowly into Philadelphia. On May twenty-fourth, Rufus King wrote home that he was "mortified" because he alone was from New England. "The backwardness may prove unfortunate. Pray hurry on your delegates." New Hampshire delayed because she had no money in her treasury to pay expenses; it was nearly August when two out of her four appointees appeared. One of them, John Langdon, was a rich merchant from Portsmouth, formerly president of his state, described as a "large handsome man, and of a very noble bearing, who courted popularity with the zeal of a lover and the constancy of a martyr." Rhode Island stayed away. At Providence the agrarian party controlled the legislature; they had even contrived to pass a law punishing with fines any creditor who refused the inflationary state currency. It was common knowledge that certain politicians were feathering their nests under the system. A strong central government no doubt would force debts to be paid in specie: Rhode Island at the moment would have none of it. *Rogue Island*, a Boston newspaper called her in disgust, recommending that she "be dropped out of the Union or apportioned to the different States which surround her.". . .

James Madison

James Madison rode over to the Convention from New York, where he had been sitting in Congress. It was typical of Madison to arrive in Philadelphia eleven days early; this was a man who liked to be ready. Long study had given him a prophetic quality; in a letter to Washington as early as April he had outlined the most important points that were to be debated in the Convention. Madison was a small man, slight of figure, "no bigger," someone said, "than half a piece of soap." He had a quiet voice. In meetings, members called out, asking him to speak louder, or the clerk omitted parts of his speeches, "because he spoke low and could not be heard." To his friends he was Jemmy.

But Madison, enormously pertinacious, was also flexible—two qualities not often found together. Of the entire delegation no one came better prepared intellectually. At his request Jefferson (eight years his senior) had sent books from Paris. Madison asked for "whatever may throw light on the general constitution and *droit public* of the several confederacies which have existed." The books arrived not by ones and twos but by the hundred: thirty-seven volumes of the new *Encyclopédie Méthodique*, books on political theory and the law of nations, histories, works by Burlamiqui, Voltaire, Diderot, Mably, Necker, d'Albon. There were biographies and memoirs, histories in sets of eleven volumes and such timely productions as Mirabeau on *The Order of the Cincinnati*. In return Madison sent grafts of American trees for Jefferson to show in France, pecan nuts, pippin apples, cranberries, though he failed in shipping the opossums Jefferson asked for, and the "pair of Virginia redbirds." Madison threw himself into a study of confederacies ancient and modern, wrote out a long essay comparing governments, with each analysis followed by a section of his own, entitled "Vices of the Political System of the United States." "Let the national government be armed with a positive and complete authority in all cases where uniform measures are necessary. Let it have a negative, in all cases whatsoever, on the legislative acts of the states, as the King of Great Britain heretofore had. Let this national supremacy be extended also to the judiciary department."

Small wonder that James Madison, in his methodical way, was to be the most formidable adversary the Virginia anti-Constitutionalists would encounter, especially the inflammable Patrick Henry. Madison knew the politics of his state as Hamilton knew them in New York, knew also that the actual writing of a constitution was only one step in a long and hazardous process. Madison understood the meaning and procedure of that Revolutionary discovery, the constituent convention. Already he had set down his ideas in letters to his friends. First, the states must appoint delegates. Then the convention must reach agreement and sign a document. Thirdly, the document would be submitted to Congress. If Congress approved, the states would be invited to call their separate ratification conventions, which meant that technically, the Philadelphia Convention sat in a position merely advisory.

Yet should it fail, what hope was there of calling another? In April, a full month before the Convention met, Madison had told a Virginia colleague that the nearer the crisis approached, the more he trembled for the issue. "The necessity," he wrote, "of gaining the concurrence of the Convention in some system that will answer the purpose, the subsequent approbation of Congress, and the final sanction of the states, presents a series of chances which would inspire despair in any case where the alternative was less formidable."

It was like Madison to declare that the situation was too serious for despair. It was like Washington, too, of whom the British historian Trevelyan was to write that he "had learned the inmost secret of the brave, who train themselves to contemplate in mind the worst that can happen and in thought resign themselves—but in action resign themselves never." At fifty-five, Washington was almost a generation older than Madison. Yet the two had known each other for years; Madison had been in the Virginia government since '76. It is hard to say which man was the more serious by nature. Reading Madison's long letters on politics, with their cool forceful arguments, or Washington's with their stately rhythm, one senses beneath the elaborate paragraphs a very fury of concern for the country. And one takes comfort in this solemnity. One rejoices that these men felt no embarrassment at being persistently, at times awkwardly serious, according to their natures.

The Atlantic Revolutions: From America to Europe

Jacques Godechot

French historian Jacques Godechot has written several works on the French Revolution, including *Counter-Revolution: Doctrine and Action, 1789–1804*. In the following selection, Godechot focuses on the late eighteenth century and shows that America's revolutionary ideas spread not only to France, but Britain and Ireland as well.

The reactions of the countries of Europe to the American revolution were varied. There was passionate controversy in England, Ireland, and the United Provinces; sometimes adversaries and partisans of the revolution even came to blows. Great Britain just missed having a revolution, while one actually broke out in the United Provinces. In Belgium, France, Germany, and Switzerland it was the educated public which first became interested in the American events, but they gradually became widely known among the people. The American revolution was not the cause of immediate disorders but had long-term effects. In Italy enthusiasm for Franklin and the democratic institutions of the United States developed only in 1796. Although Spain, like France and Holland, participated in the American war of independence, it seems to have remained rather indifferent to the American revolution. In Eastern Europe, Poland, and Russia, the *intelligentsia* kept informed of the events in America, but they were only a very small fraction of the population and were scarcely able to transmit the American ideals to illiterate masses.

Reprinted with the permission of The Free Press, a division of Simon & Schuster, Inc., from *France and the Atlantic Revolution of the Eighteenth Century, 1770–1799*, by Jacques Godechot. Translated by Herbert H. Rowen. Copyright ©1965 by The Free Press.

Revolutionary Thought in Great Britain

The American revolution led to a series of revolutionary disorders—sometimes of extremely grave character—in Great Britain, particularly in Ireland and in Yorkshire, as well as in London itself, between 1778 and 1781. If the various disturbances did not degenerate into a revolution, it was because they displayed different characteristics and had different origins. . . .

The disorders began in 1778 in Ireland. They were consequences of the American revolution and even more of the political and social organization of the island. As is known, the subjugation of Ireland by England was made tighter in the eighteenth century. The Irish Catholics, who formed a majority of the population, possessed few political rights and little land. The soil belonged almost completely to Protestants of English or Scottish extraction or to the Anglican "Church of Ireland." But the Irish Protestants themselves did not enjoy the same rights as Englishmen. Although they were represented by a majority of members in the Dublin Parliament, that assembly was subordinated to the Parliament in Westminster and was not its equal. The inhabitants of Ireland, Protestant as well as Catholic, accordingly had many reasons for discontent. When the English colonies of America revolted against the mother country, the Irish saw in the American insurrection both example and encouragement. The war in America had other repercussions in Ireland. It caused a reduction in Irish exports to the American continent and an economic crisis soon resulted. Furthermore, Ireland itself seemed threatened by attack from the American rebels. In 1778 the American privateer John Paul Jones made a raid on Belfast which aroused great anxiety. In addition, the French were preparing in Normandy a landing operation in Great Britain; Ireland seemed to be the target, as it had been during earlier Anglo-French wars.

The British government, which had sent most of its troops to America, decided to raise volunteers to defend Ireland. It called upon the Protestants in 1778, but their numbers were insufficient and Catholics had to be admitted into the ranks of the militia in 1779. The Irish Volunteers, who numbered 40,000 in 1779 and 80,000 in 1782, quickly became aware of their strength and began to demand reforms and increased liberty. They organized a boycott of English goods in imitation of the American rebels. Under the leadership of Grattan, a member of its lower house, the Dublin Parliament granted a subsidy to the King of England for only six months. In the House of Commons at Westminster the Irish were defended by the same men who had stood up for the rebels in America, notably Edmund Burke. The English government made some concessions. The Test Bill, which excluded Catholics from all public office, was repealed for Ireland; the Irish Parliament was declared autonomous; and the two kingdoms of Great Britain and Ireland were proclaimed equal. These concessions did not satisfy the Irish. In November 1783 they held a Grand National Convention in Dublin; it demanded that Irish Catholics be given the right to vote and that elections to the Dublin Parliament be held every three years. The Protestants of Ireland became frightened and the Irish Parliament rejected these demands. The war in America had just ended, and the British government was now able to send troops to Ireland. The Irish Catholics took refuge in clandestine activity, forming the secret society of the "United Irishmen," which adopted the demands formulated by the Dublin convention as the basis of its program.

Riots in England

While these events were occurring in Ireland, other events provoked by similar causes were taking place in England. Just as the revolt of the American colonists had incited the Irish to demand reforms, so it impelled some Englishmen to propose profound changes in British institutions. In 1780 John Jebb, a Whig, published a series of political demands which formed the basis of the program of the "Radicals" for almost a century. These demands included universal male suffrage, secrecy of the ballot, annual election of Parliaments, equal constituencies, with the number of members proportional to the population, salaries for members of Parliament, and eligibility of all voters to the House of Commons. "Associations" were formed to achieve these demands; they were especially numerous in London and Yorkshire, and the agitation became known as the "Yorkshire movement." It was essentially a movement of the bourgeoisie, but it developed an atmosphere of clamor and uncertainty which engendered extremely serious popular disturbances—the Gordon Riots in London in June 1780.

Although originally the goals of the London rioters were diametrically opposed to the objectives being sought by the Catholics in Ireland and the English Radicals, the London disorders were nonetheless part of the great revolutionary movement of the West. The Londoners rose at the call of Lord George Gordon, president of an association seeking repeal of the Catholic Relief Bill which Parliament had passed in 1778. This law, which was valid only for England and Wales, revoked a statute passed under William III which condemned Catholic schoolteachers to life imprisonment and the loss of the right to inherit land. In exchange for this minimal concession, the Catholics were to swear an oath of loyalty to the King and renounce recourse to any papal jurisdiction. This law had already caused disorders in Scotland; on February 2, 1779, two Catholic chapels were destroyed at Edinburgh and Catholic homes and shops were looted. The demand of the Irish Catholics for abolition of the Test Act, and the successes won by France and Spain—Catholic countries—in the American war increased the anxiety and discontent of the London people. The riots therefore seemed to be at first an attack upon the principle of religious toleration advocated by the philosophes. But, as we shall see, the riot soon degenerated into a revolt against the rich and the government which protected them. From this point of view the Gordon Riots closely resembled the great riots which marked the revolution in the West, particularly in France and Italy.

The riots began on June 2, 1780. Lord George Gordon had urged the Londoners to present to Parliament a petition demanding repeal of the Catholic Relief Act. He declared that if fewer than 20,000 persons were present, he would resign as president of the association organized to obtain the withdrawal of the law. A crowd estimated at no less than 30,000 demonstrators, perhaps as many as 60,000, crowded the streets to accompany the petition, which bore 44,000 signatures. The prime minister, Lord North, was jeered, along with Edmund Burke, the defender of the American rebels, who was considered to be favorable to the Catholics. When despite the demonstration the members of Commons decided to adjourn discussion of the petition, the crowd broke loose. It began to destroy Catholic chapels and to attack the homes of Catholics. The disorders did not cease with nightfall and were renewed on June 3, 4, and 5. On the sixth, the demonstrators were attacked by cavalry and forthwith turned their fury against the representatives of authority. The home of a judge and a police station were destroyed, the brand new prison of Old Bailey was burned down and its prisoners set free. On June 7 many other prisons were attacked and their gates opened. Numerous homes of nobles and rich businessmen were threatened. On the evening of Wednesday, June 7, thirty-six gigantic fires lit the sky of London; nothing comparable was to take place in Paris during the entire revolution. On June 8, when the venerable Bank of England was attacked, the burghers of London took up arms and formed a militia. On June 9 Lord George Gordon, along with numerous rioters, was arrested and imprisoned. Tried for high treason, Lord Gordon was defended by the Whig barrister, Thomas Erskine, and acquitted on February 5, 1781. In all, the riots caused 210 deaths and 248 wounded, including 75 who died in hospitals. The police made 450 arrests. One hundred and sixty persons were tried, 62 sentenced to death, and 25 hanged, including four women and a youth of 16. Thirty-two private homes were completely wrecked and 110 persons were reimbursed for losses amounting to a total of £30,000. Statistics on the occupations of the persons arrested show that 70 percent were wage-earners. It is apparent that this uprising was essentially provoked by economic difficulties caused by a rapid increase in population, a greater increase in prices than in wages, and the trade stagnation caused by the war in America. Characteristic was the reply given by an arrested rioter when it was pointed out that he had attacked the home of a Protestant: "Protestant or not, no one needs more than £10,000 a year—that's enough for anyone to live on." The attack upon the prisons must be interpreted as the expression of a vague aspiration for greater social justice. Hostility against the Catholics was only a pretext for the riots. If the demands of the bourgeois Radicals had had a social and not an exclusively political character, they perhaps might have been able to attract the discontented farmers and workers. Then a revolution would have occurred in England. But as a whole the British bourgeoisie were satisfied, for they had had a share in government since the revolutions of 1640 and 1688. They did not seek an alliance with the lower classes, as the French bourgeoisie did a few years later. In England the interests of the bourgeoisie and the lower classes were already extremely divergent by the end of the eighteenth century; they did not suffer, as in America, from the common oppression of a distant and almost foreign government, nor, as in France, from a still powerful feudal regime. Abolition of a few sinecures, some budgetary economies, the collective resignation of the North ministry, and above all the conclusion of peace with the United States were sufficient to satisfy them. Nonetheless the revolutionary movement was not dead. After the revolution developed in France, it reappeared in England.

Appendix

Excerpts from Original Documents Pertaining to the American Revolution

Document 1: Government Founded on Our Natures

James Otis's Rights of the Colonies asserted and proved *was one of the first written declarations of colonial rights. Issued in pamphlet form, it became one of the most widely read political documents in the 1760s.*

The same omniscient, omnipotent, infinitely good and gracious Creator of the universe, who has been pleased to make it necessary that what we call matter should gravitate, for the celestial bodies to roll round their axes, dance their orbits and perform their various revolutions in that beautiful order and concert, which we all admire, has made it equally necessary that from Adam and Eve to these degenerate days, the different sexes should sweetly attract each other, form societies of single families, of which larger bodies and communities are as naturally, mechanically, and necessarily combined, as the dew of Heaven and the soft distilling rain is collected by the all enliv'ning heat of the sun. Government is therefore most evidently founded on the necessities of our nature. It is by no means an arbitrary thing, depending merely on compact or human will for its existence. . . .

'The natural liberty of man is to be free from any superior power on earth, and not to be under the will or legislative authority of man, but only to have the law of nature for his rule.' This is the liberty of independent states; this is the liberty of every man out of society, and who has a mind to live so; which liberty is only abridged in certain instances, not lost to those who are born in or voluntarily enter into society; this gift of God cannot be annihilated.

The Colonists being men, have a right to be considered as equally entitled to all the rights of nature with the Europeans, and they are not to be restrained in the exercise of any of these rights, but for the evident good of the whole community. By being or becoming members of society, they have not renounced their natural liberty in any greater degree than other good citizens, and if 'tis taken from them without their consent, they are so far enslaved.

Samuel Eliot Morison, *Sources and Documents Illustrating the American Revolution, 1764–1788, and the Formation of the Federal Constitution.* London: Oxford University Press, 1929.

Document 2: "The Stamp Papers Burn"

The Stamp Act caused widespread protest in the American colonies. Some made themselves heard through established political forums; others staged raucous demonstrations. The following is a popular song of the period written about a Stamp Act riot.

Let us Make wise Resolves and to them stand strong
Your Puffs and your Vapours will Ne'er last Long
To Ma[i]ntain Our Just Rights, Every Measure Pursue
To Our King we'll be Loyal, To Ourselves we'll be True.

Those Blessings Our Fathers, Obtain'd by their Blood
We are Justly Oblig'd to Our sons to make Good
All Internal Taxes let us then Nobly spurn
These Effigy's First, The Next The Stamp Papers Burn.

Chorus

Sing Tantarara, Burn All, Burn All
Sing Tantarara, Burn All.

Stanley I. Kutler, *Looking for America: The People's History*. Vol. 1. New York: W.W. Norton, 1979.

Document 3: Resolutions of the Stamp Act Congress

The Stamp Act Congress was convened to draft a formal colonial response to the Scamp Act. In the following resolutions, excerpted here, the delegates reassert their right as Englishmen to representation in Parliament.

I. That His Majesty's subjects in these colonies owe the same allegiance to the Crown of Great Britain that is owning from his subjects born within the realm, and all due subordination to that august body the Parliament of Great Britain.

II. That His Majesty's liege subjects in these colonies are intitled to all the inherent rights and liberties of his natural born subjects within the kingdom of Great Britain.

III. That it is inseparably essential to the freedom of a people, and the undoubted right of Englishmen, that no taxes be imposed on them but with their own consent, given personally or by their representatives.

IV. That the people of these colonies are not, and from their local circumstances cannot be, represented in the House of Commons in Great Britain.

V. That the only representatives of the people of these colonies are persons chosen therein by themselves, and that no taxes ever have been, or can be constitutionally imposed on them, but by their respective legislatures.

VI. That all supplies to the Crown being free gifts of the people, it is unreasonable and inconsistent with the principles and spirit of the British Constitution, for the people of Great Britain to grant to His Majesty the property of the colonists.

VII. That trial by jury is the inherent and invaluable right of every British subject in these colonies.

VIII. That the late Act of Parliament, entitled *An Act for granting and applying certain stamp duties, and other duties, in the British colonies and plantations in America, etc.*, by imposing taxes on the inhabitants of these colonies; and the said Act, and several other Acts, by extending the jurisdiction of the courts of Admiralty beyond its ancient limits, have a manifest tendency to subvert the rights and liberties of the colonists.

IX. That the duties imposed by several late Acts of Parliament, from the peculiar circumstances of these colonies, will be extremely burthensome and grievous; and from the scarcity of specie, the payment of them absolutely impracticable.

X. That as the profits of the trade of these colonies ultimately center in Great Britain, to pay for the manufactures which they are obliged to take from thence, they eventually contribute very largely to all supplies granted there to the Crown.

XI. That the restrictions imposed by several late Acts of Parliament on the trade of these colonies will render them unable to purchase the manufactures of Great Britain.

XII. That the increase, prosperity, and happiness of these colonies depend on the full and free enjoyments of their rights and liberties, and an intercourse with Great Britain mutually affectionate and advantageous.

XIII. That it is the right of the British subjects in these colonies to petition the King or either House of Parliament.

Lastly, That it is the indispensible duty of these colonies to the best of sovereigns, to the mother country, and to themselves, to endeavour by a loyal and dutiful address to His Majesty, and humble applications to both Houses of Parliament, to procure the repeal of the Act for granting and applying certain stamp duties, of all clauses of any other Acts of Parliament, whereby the jurisdiction of the Admiralty is extended as aforesaid, and of the other late Acts for the restriction of American commerce.

Samuel Eliot Morison, *Sources and Documents Illustrating the American Revolution, 1764–1788, and the Formation of the Federal Constitution*. London: Oxford University Press, 1929.

Document 4: The Levellers

Thwarted in civil opposition to the Stamp Act, many Americans came to believe that public protest was the best way to show their displeasure. The following notices describe rioting against New York officials over land rights in 1766. The rioters, who claimed their rights as Englishmen were being usurped, organized themselves into a group called the Levellers.

APRIL 29, 1766.

The city, alarmed from the approach of the country Levellers, called the Westchester men. The militia ordered to hold themselves in readiness. Letters received from them in town declaring that if Mr. Cortlandt does not give them a grant forever to his lands, they will march with their body now collected and pull down his house in town and also one belonging to Mr. Lambert Moore. . . .

MAY 6, 1766.

Proclamation issued 100£ reward for the taking of Pendergrast, chief of the country Levellers and 50£ for either Munro and Finch, two officers.

JUNE 28, 1766.

Advices from the Manor of Livingston that the Levellers have rose there to the number of 500 men, 200 of which had marched to murder the lord of the manor and level his house, unless he would sign leases for 'em agreeable to their form, as theirs were now expired, and that they would neither pay rent, taxes, etc., nor suffer other tenants. The Levellers met by Mr. Walter Livingston, the son, who made a sally with 40 armed men—the 200 having only sticks—obliged them to retire, not without their threatening a more respectable visit on the return of Colonel Livingston of the Manor.

JUNE 29, 1766.

Seventeen hundred of the Levellers with firearms are collected at Poughkeepsie. All the jails broke open through all the counties this side of Albany, of the east side of the river, by people headed by Pendergrast. Eight thousand cartridges sent up to the 28th Regt. . . .

AUGUST 6, 1766.

Accounts from the Circuit, Pendergrast is indicted for high treason.

AUGUST 19, 1766.

Wm. Pendergrast, who was tried at Poughkeepsie and found guilty of high treason and received sentence of death, begged leave of the court to admit him to deliver a few words, viz: "That if opposition to government was deemed rebellion, no member of that court were entitled to set upon his trial."

From "Journals of Captain John Montresor, 1757–1778,"
New-York Historical Society, Collections, XIV.

"Journals of Captain John Montresor, 1757–1778," in Milton Meltzer, ed., <i>The American Revolutionaries: A History in Their Own Words, 1750–1800.</i> New York: Thomas Y. Crowell, 1987.

Document 5: Fighting the Scavengers

The Boston Tea Party was an act of rebellion against British authority in Boston. The following is excerpted from an eyewitness account by a participant.

In about three hours from the time we went on board, we had thus broken and thrown overboard every tea chest to be found in the ship, while those in the other ships were disposing of the tea in the same way, at the same time. We were surrounded by British armed ships, but no attempt was made to resist us.

We then quietly retired to our several places of residence, without having any conversation with each other, or taking any measures to discover who were our associates; nor do I recollect of our having had the knowledge of the name of a single individual concerned in that affair, except that of Leonard Pitt, the commander of my division, whom I have mentioned. There appeared to be an understanding that each individual should volunteer his services, keep his own secret, and risk the consequences for himself. No disorder took place during that transaction, and it was observed at that time that the stillest night ensued that Boston had enjoyed for many months.

During the time we were throwing the tea overboard, there were several attempts made by some of the citizens of Boston and its vicinity to carry off small quantities of it for their family use. To effect that object, they would watch their opportunity to snatch up a handful from the deck, where it became plentifully scattered, and put it into their pockets. One Captain O'Connor, whom I well knew, came on board for that purpose, and when he supposed he was not noticed, filled his pockets, and also the lining of his coat. But I had detected him and gave information to the captain of what he was doing. We were ordered to take him into custody, and just as he was stepping from the vessel, I seized him by the skirt of his coat, and attempting to pull him back, I tore it off; but, springing forward, by a rapid effort he made his escape. He had, however, to run a gauntlet through the crowd upon the wharf, each one, as he passed, giving him a kick or a stroke.

Another attempt was made to save a little tea from the ruins of the cargo by a tall, aged man who wore a large cocked hat and white wig, which was fashionable at that time. He had sleightly slipped a little into his pocket, but being detected, they seized him and, taking his hat and wig from his head, threw them, together with the tea, of which they had emptied his pockets, into the water. In consideration of his advanced age, he was permitted to escape, with now and then a slight kick.

The next morning, after we had cleared the ships of the tea, it was discovered that very considerable quantities of it were floating upon the surface of the water; and to prevent the possibility of any of its being saved for use, a number of small boats were manned by sailors and citizens, who rowed them into those parts of the harbor wherever the tea was visible, and by beating it with oars and paddles so thoroughly drenched it as to render its entire destruction inevitable.

Stanley I. Kutler, *Looking for America: The People's History*. Vol. 1. New York: W.W. Norton, 1979.

Document 6: "No Damage . . . Except to the Tea"

Many of the participants in the Boston Tea Party recorded the event as a celebrated exploit. Here, Robert Sessions recounts his activities that fateful night.

I was living in Boston at the time, in the family of a Mr. Davis, a lumber merchant, as a common laborer. On that eventful evening, when Mr. Davis came in from the town meeting, I asked him what was to be done with the tea.

"They are now throwing it overboard," he replied.

Receiving permission, I went immediately to the spot. Everything was as light as day, by the means of lamps and torches—a pin might be seen lying on the wharf. I went on board where they were at work, and took hold with my own hands.

I was not one of those appointed to destroy the tea, and who disguised themselves as Indians, but was a volunteer, the disguised men being largely men of family and position in Boston, while I was a young man whose home and relations were in Connecticut. The appointed and disguised party proving too small for the quick work necessary, other young men, similarly circumstanced with myself, joined them in their labors.

The chests were drawn up by a tackle—one man bringing them forward in the hold, another putting a rope around them, and others hoisting them to the deck and carrying them to the vessel's side. The chests were then opened, the tea emptied over the side, and the chests thrown overboard.

Perfect regularity prevailed during the whole transaction. Although there were many people on the wharf, entire silence prevailed—no clamor, no talking. Nothing was meddled with but the teas on board.

After having emptied the hold, the deck was swept clean, and everything put in its proper place. An officer on board was requested to come up from the cabin and see that no damage was done except to the tea.

From Milton Meltzer, ed., *The American Revolutionaries: A History in Their Own Words, 1750–1800*. New York: Thomas Y. Crowell, 1987.

Document 7: A Proposal for Cooperation

James Galloway was one of the more moderate members of the Continental Congress. He felt that some measure of cooperation between the colonies and Parliament was possible in the form of a grand council. His proposition, excerpted here, failed to gather enough votes but shows that colonial leaders disagreed on a course of action as late as 1774.

A Plan of a proposed Union between Great Britain and the Colonies of . . .

That a British and American Legislature, for regulating the administration of the general affairs of America, be proposed and established in America, including all the said colonies; within and under which government, each colony shall retain its present constitution and powers of regulating and governing its own internal police in all cases whatsoever.

That the said government be administered by a President-General to be appointed by the King, and a Grand Council to be chosen by the representatives of the people of the several colonies in their respective Assemblies, once in every three years.

That the several Assemblies shall choose members for the Grand Council in the following proportions, viz.: . . . who shall meet at the city of———for the first time, being called by the President-General as soon as conveniently may be after his appointment. That there shall be a new election of members for the Grand Council every three years; and on the death, removal, or resignation of any member, his place shall be supplied by a new choice at the next sitting of Assembly of the colony he represented.

That the Grand Council shall meet once in every year if they think it necessary, and oftener if occasions shall require, at such time and place as they shall adjourn to at the last preceding meeting, or as they shall be called to meet at, by the President-General on any emergency.

That the Grand Council shall have power to choose their Speaker, and shall hold and exercise all the like rights, liberties, and privileges as are held and exercised by and in the House of Commons of Great Britain.

That the President-General shall hold his office during the pleasure of the King, and his assent shall be requisite to all Acts of the Grand Council, and it shall be his office and duty to cause them to be carried into execution.

That the President-General, by and with the advice and consent of the Grand Council, hold and exercise all the legislative rights, powers, and authorities, necessary for regulating and administering all the general police and affairs of the colonies, in which Great Britain and the colonies, or any of them, the colonies in general, or more than one colony, are in any manner concerned, as well civil and criminal as commercial.

That the said President-General and Grand Council be an inferior and distinct branch of the British Legislature, united and incorporated with it for the aforesaid general purposes; and that any of the said general regulations may originate, and be formed and digested, either in the Parliament of Great Britain or in the said Grand Council; and being prepared, transmitted to the other for their approbation or dissent; and that the assent of both shall be requisite to the validity of all such general Acts and Statutes.

That in time of war, all bills for granting aids to the Crown, prepared by the Grand Council and approved by the President-General, shall be valid and passed into a law, without the assent of the British Parliament.

Samuel Eliot Morison, *Sources and Documents Illustrating the American Revolution, 1764–1788, and the Formation of the Federal Constitution.* London: Oxford University Press, 1929.

Document 8: An Account of the Battle of Lexington

The Patriots hailed the Battles of Lexington and Concord as victories. The British hardly considered them battles. The following excerpt is taken from a quote by a minuteman at the Battle of Lexington.

Immediately upon their appearing so suddenly and so nigh, Capt. Parker, who commanded the militia company, ordered the men to disperse and take care of themselves, and not to fire. Upon this, our men dispersed—but many of them not so speedily as they might have done, not having the most distant idea of such brutal barbarity and more than savage cruelty from the troops of a British king, as they immediately experienced! For, no sooner did they come in sight of our company, but one of them, supposed to be an officer of rank, was heard to say to the troops, "Damn them! We will have them!" Upon which the troops shouted aloud, huzza'd, and rushed furiously towards our men.

About the same time, three officers (supposed to be Col. Smith, Major Pitcairn and another officer) advanced on horse back to the front of the body, and coming within 5 or 6 rods of the militia, one of them cried out, "Ye villains, ye Rebels, disperse! Damn you, disperse!"—or words to this effect. One of them (whether the same or not is not easily determined) said, "Lay down your arms! Damn you, why don't you lay down your arms?" The second of these officers, about this time, fired a pistol towards the militia as they were dispersing. The foremost, who was within a few yards of our men, brandishing his sword and then pointing towards them, with a loud voice said to the troops, "Fire! By God, fire!"—which was instantly followed by a discharge of arms from the said troops, succeeded by a very heavy and close fire upon our party, dispersing, so long as any of them were within reach. Eight were left dead upon the ground! Ten were wounded. The rest of the company, through divine goodness, were (to a miracle) preserved unhurt in this murderous action! . . .

One circumstance more before the brigade quitted Lexington, I beg leave to mention, as what may give a further specimen of the spirit and character of the officers and men of this body of troops. After the militia company were dispersed and the firing ceased, the troops drew up and formed a body on the common, fired a volley and gave three huzzas, by way of triumph and as expressive of the joy of victory and glory of conquest! Of this transaction, I was a witness, having, at that time, a fair view of their motions and being at the distance of not more than 70 or 80 rods from them.

Stanley I. Kutler, *Looking for America: The People's History*. Vol. 1. New York: W.W. Norton, 1979.

Document 9: Skirmishes at Concord and Lexington

The minutemen of Massachusetts were the first to see action during the skirmishes at Concord and Lexington. A young shoemaker, Sylvanus Wood, recalled the historic event.

I immediately arose, took my gun, and with Robert Douglass went in haste to Lexington. When I arrived there, I inquired of Captain Parker the news. Parker told me he did not know what to believe, for a man had come up about half an hour before and informed him that the British troops were not on the road. But while we were talking, a messenger came up and told the captain that the British troops were within half a mile. Parker immediately turned to his drummer, and ordered him to beat to arms. . . .

The British troops approached us rapidly in platoons, with a general officer on horseback at their head. The officer came up to within about two rods of the center of the company where I stood, the first platoon being about three rods distant. There they halted. The officer then swung his sword, and said, "Lay down your arms, you damned rebels, or you are all dead men—Fire!" Some guns were fired by the British at us from the first platoon, but no person was killed or hurt, being probably charged only with powder.

Just at this time, Captain Parker ordered every man to take care of himself. The company immediately dispersed; and while the company was dispersing and leaping over the wall, the second platoon of the British fired, and killed some of our men. There was not a gun fired by any of Captain Parker's company, within my knowledge. I was so situated that I must have known it, had anything of the kind taken place before a total dispersion of our company. I have been intimately acquainted with the inhabitants of Lexington, and particularly with those of Captain Parker's company, and on one occasion, and with one exception, I have never heard any of them say or pretend that there was any firing at the British from Parker's company, or any individual in it.

From *Battles of the United States by Sea and Land*,
Henry B. Dawson, 1858

From Milton Meltzer, ed., *The American Revolutionaries: A History in Their Own Words, 1750–1800.* New York: Thomas Y. Crowell, 1987.

Document 10: The British View

The British army's view of the first battles of the American Revolution is very different from the Patriots' view. Here, British lieutenant Frederick Mackenzie describes the march from Concord back to Boston.

During the whole of the march from Lexington the rebels kept an incessant irregular fire from all points at the column, which was the more galling as our flanking parties which at first were placed at sufficient distances to cover the march of it were at last, from the different obstructions they occasionally met with, obliged to keep almost close to it.

Our men had very few opportunities of getting good shots at

the rebels, as they hardly ever fired but under cover of a stone wall, from behind a tree, or out of a house, and the moment they had fired, they lay down out of sight until they had loaded again or the column had passed. In the road, indeed, in our rear, they were most numerous and came on pretty close, frequently calling out "King Hancock forever!" Many of them were killed in the houses on the roadside from whence they fired; in some of them seven or eight men were destroyed. Some houses were forced open in which no person could be discovered, but when the column had passed, numbers sallied out from some place in which they had lain concealed, fired at our rear guard, and augmented the numbers which followed us.

If we had had time to set fire to those houses, many rebels must have perished in them, but as night drew on Lord Percy thought it best to continue the march. Many houses were plundered by the soldiers, notwithstanding the efforts of the officers to prevent it. I have no doubt this inflamed the rebels and made many of them follow us farther than they would otherwise have done. By all accounts some soldiers who stayed too long in the houses were killed in the very act of plundering by those who lay concealed in them. We brought in about ten prisoners, some of whom were taken in arms. One or two more were killed on the march while prisoners by the fire of their own people.

From Milton Meltzer, ed., *The American Revolutionaries: A History in Their Own Words, 1750–1800.* New York: Thomas Y. Crowell, 1987.

Document 11: *Common Sense*

One of the most powerful documents of the revolutionary era was Common Sense *by Thomas Paine. Paine, a recent immigrant from England, summarized colonial discontent.*

Britain is the parent country say some. Then the more shame upon her conduct. Even brutes do not devour their young, nor savages make war upon their families. . . . Europe and not England is the parent country of America. This New World has been the asylum for the persecuted lovers of civil and religious liberty from every part of Europe. Hither have they fled, not from the tender embraces of the mother, but from the cruelty of the monster; and it is so far true of England that the same tyranny which drove the first emigrants from home pursues their descendants still. . . .

America is only a secondary object in the system of British politics. England consults the good of this country no further than it answers her own purpose. Wherefore, her own interest leads her to suppress the growth of ours in every case which doth not promote her advantage, or in the least interferes with it. . . .

It is unreasonable to suppose that France or Spain will give us any kind of assistance, if we mean only to make use of that assistance for the purpose of repairing the breach and strengthening the connection between Britain and America; because, those powers would be sufferers by the consequences.

While we profess ourselves the subjects of Britain, we must, in the eyes of foreign nations, be considered as Rebels.

From Milton Meltzer, ed., *The American Revolutionaries: A History in Their Own Words, 1750–1800*. New York: Thomas Y. Crowell, 1987.

Document 12: Rascally Stupidity

Life in the Continental Army was most bitter during the winter. With little food and inadequate supplies, Washington and his army struggled to survive. Local farmers and merchants hesitated to help for fear of British discovery and punishment. One soldier wrote this letter to his brother, pleading for help.

The rascally stupidity which now prevails in the country at large is beyond all descriptions. They patiently see our illustrious commander at the head of twenty-five hundred or three thousand ragged, though virtuous and good, men and be obliged to put up with what no troops ever did before.

Why don't you reinforce your army, feed them, clothe, and pay them? Why do you suffer the enemy to have a foothold on the continent? You can prevent it. Send your men to the field, believe you are Americans, not suffer yourselves to be duped into the thought that the French will relieve you and fight your battles. It is your own superiorness that induced Congress to ask foreign aid. It is a reflection too much for a soldier. You don't deserve to be free men, unless you can believe it yourselves. When they arrive, they will not put up with such treatment as your army have done. They will not serve week after week without meat, without clothing, and paid in filthy rags.

I despise my countrymen. I wish I could say I was not born in America. I once gloried in it, but am now ashamed of it. If you do your duty, though late, you may finish the war this campaign. You must immediately fill your regiments and pay your troops in hard monies. They cannot exist as soldiers otherwise. The insults and neglect which the army have met with from the country beggars all description. It must go no farther; they can endure it no longer. I have wrote in a passion. Indeed, I am scarce ever free from it . . . and all this for my cowardly countrymen who flinch at the very time when their exertions are wanted and hold their purse strings as though they would damn the world rather than part with a dollar to their army.

From Milton Meltzer, ed., *The American Revolutionaries: A History in Their Own Words, 1750–1800.* New York: Thomas Y. Crowell, 1987.

Document 13: From a Military Journal

Army discipline during the Revolution matched the times, brutish and violent. Desertion was common, and its penalty ranged from lashes, to life in prison, to death. The following is excerpted from the testimony of James Thacher, a surgeon's mate, who witnessed such punishments.

The culprit being securely tied to a tree or post receives on his naked back the number of lashes assigned him, by a whip formed of several small knotted cords, which sometimes cut through the skin at every stroke. However strange it may appear, a soldier will often receive the severest stripe without uttering a groan or once shrieking from the lash, even while the blood flows freely form his lacerated wounds. This must be ascribed to stubbornness or pride. They have, however, adopted a method which they say mitigates the anguish in some measure. It is by putting between the teeth a leaden bullet, on which they chew while under the lash, till it is made quite flat and jagged. In some instances of incorrigible villains, it is adjudged by the court that the culprit receive his punishment at several different times, a certain number of stripes repeated at intervals of two or three days, in which case the wounds are in a state of inflammation and the skin rendered more sensibly tender, and the terror of the punishment is greatly aggravated.

From Milton Meltzer, ed., *The American Revolutionaries: A History in Their Own Words, 1750–1800.* New York: Thomas Y. Crowell, 1987.

Document 14: Prisoners of War

American and British prisoners of war alike endured deplorable conditions. Here an American officer describes the place that was his prison for more than six months.

I arrived at the jail in Philadelphia about eight o'clock in the evening. I was locked into a cold room destitute of everything but cold stone walls and bare floors—no kind of a seat to sit on—all total darkness, no water to drink or a morsel to eat; destitute a blanket to cover me, I groped about my solitary cell, and in moving about I found that there were two or three persons lying on the floor asleep. I said nothing to them, nor they to me. I stood on my feet and leaned back against the wall, and sometimes moved about the room, and then to change my position I sat on the floor, but no sleep nor slumber; parched with thirst and no one on which I could call for a drop of water. In short, it was a long, dismal, dreary and most gloomy night that I ever beheld.

I reflected on the miseries of the damn'd in that eternal, friendless prison of despair, but still hope hovered around my soul that I should see another morning. Morning finally arrived, and at a late hour, we were furnished with some very hard sea bread and salted pork, and I was able to obtain some water to drink. Being altogether moneyless I could purchase nothing for my comfort. I pretty soon sold my watch for half its value, and with the money I received for it I was able to procure some food pleasant to my taste. I wholly gave up my allowance of provisions to the poor soldiers.

At this time and in this jail were confined 700 prisoners of war. A few small rooms were sequestered for the officers. Each room must contain sixteen men, we fully covered the whole floor when we lay down to sleep, and the poor soldiers were shut into rooms of the same magnitude with double the number. The poor soldiers were soon seized with the jailfever, as it was called, and it swept off in the course of three months 400 men, who were all buried in one continued grave without coffins. The length of a man was the width of the grave, lying three deep one upon another. I thus lived in jail from the 5th of October 1777, till the month of May 1778. Our number daily decreasing by the King of Terrors. Such a scene of mortality I never witnessed before. Death was so frequent that it ceased to terrify. It ceased to warn; it ceased to alarm survivors.

From Milton Meltzer, ed., *The American Revolutionaries: A History in Their Own Words, 1750–1800*. New York: Thomas Y. Crowell, 1987.

Document 15: The Battle of Long Island

The Battle of Long Island was nearly the last for George Washington's army. Forced to retreat in the night on August 29, 1776, Washington saves his army to fight another day. Colonel Benjamin Tallmadge describes the battle and the ensuing retreat.

This was the first time in my life that I had witnessed the awful scene of a battle when man was engaged to destroy fellowman. I well remember my sensations on the occasion, for they were solemn beyond description, and very hardly could I bring my mind to be willing to attempt the life of a fellow creature. . . . Our entrenchment was so weak that it is most wonderful the British general did not attempt to storm it soon after the battle in which his troops had been victorious. . . .

It was one of the most anxious, busy nights that I ever recollect, and being the third in which hardly any of us had closed our eyes in sleep, we were all greatly fatigued. As the dawn of the next day approached, those of us who remained in the trenches became very anxious for our own safety, and when the dawn appeared there were several regiments still on duty. At this time a very dense fog began to rise, and it seemed to settle in a peculiar manner over both encampments. I recollect this peculiar providential occurrence perfectly well; and so very dense was the atmosphere that I could scarcely discern a man at six yards' distance.

When the sun rose we had just received orders to leave the lines, but before we reached the ferry, the commander in chief sent one of his aides to order the regiment to repair again to their former station on the lines. Colonel Chester immediately faced to the right about and returned, where we tarried until the sun had risen, but the fog remained as dense as ever. Finally, the second order arrived for the regiment to retire, and we very joyfully bid those trenches a long adieu. When we reached Brooklyn ferry, the boats had not returned from their last trip, but they very soon appeared and took the whole regiment over to New York; and I think I saw General Washington on the ferry stairs when I stepped into one of the last boats that received the troops. I left my horse tied to a post at the ferry.

The troops having now all safely reached New York, and the fog continuing as thick as ever, I began to think of my favorite horse and requested leave of volunteers to go with me, and guiding the boat myself, I obtained my horse and got off some distance into the river before the enemy appeared in Brooklyn.

As soon as they reached the ferry we were saluted merrily from their musketry, and finally by their field pieces; but we returned in safety. In the history of warfare I do not recollect a more fortunate retreat. After all, the providential appearance of the fog saved a part of our army from being captured, and certainly myself, among others who formed the rear guard. General Washington has never received the credit which was due to him for this wise and most fortunate measure.

From Milton Meltzer, ed., *The American Revolutionaries: A History in Their Own Words, 1750–1800.* New York: Thomas Y. Crowell, 1987.

Document 16: Black Enlistment

By 1778 the need for fresh troops led Washington and Congress to allow blacks to enlist in the Continental Army. In the Rhode Island enlistment bill, rights and privileges are carefully laid out.

WHEREAS for the preservation of the rights and liberties of the United States, it is necessary that the whole powers of government should be exerted in recruiting the Continental battalions; and whereas, His Excellency General Washington hath enclosed to this state a proposal made to him by Brigadier General Varnum, to enlist into the two battalions, raising by this state, such slaves as should be willing to enter into the service; and whereas, history affords us frequent precedents of the wisest, the freest, and bravest nations having liberated their slaves, and enlisted them as soldiers to fight in defense of their country; and also whereas, the enemy, with a great force, have taken possession of the capital, and of a greater part of this state; and this state is obliged to raise a very considerable number of troops for its own immediate defense, whereby it is in a manner rendered impossible for this state to furnish recruits for the said two battalions, without adopting the said measure so recommended.

It is voted and resolved, that every able-bodied Negro, mulatto, or Indian man slave in this state, may enlist into either of the said two battalions, to serve during the continuance of the present war with Great Britain.

That every slave, so enlisting, shall be entitled to, and receive all the bounties, wages, and encouragements, allowed by the Continental Congress, to any soldier enlisting into their service.

It is further voted and resolved, that every slave, so enlisting shall, upon his passing muster before Colonel Christopher Greene, be immediately discharged from the service of his master or mistress, and be absolutely FREE, as though he had never been encumbered with any kind of servitude or slavery.

And in case such slave shall, by sickness or otherwise, be rendered unable to maintain himself, he shall not be chargeable to his master or his mistress; but shall be supported at the expense of the state.

And whereas, slaves have been, by the laws, deemed the property of their owners, and therefore compensation ought to be made to the owners for the loss of their service;

It is further voted and resolved, that there be allowed, and paid by this state, to the owner, for every such slave so enlisting a sum according to his worth; at a price not exceeding £120 for the most valuable slave; and in proportion for a slave of less value.

From Milton Meltzer, ed., *The American Revolutionaries: A History in Their Own Words, 1750–1800.* New York: Thomas Y. Crowell, 1987.

Document 17: Atrocities to Native Americans

No place within Native American territory was safe during the war. Both British and American forces enticed Indians into fighting and then gave them no support. Some actions against Native Americans showed no conscience. This excerpt is taken from the testimony of Henry Hamilton about the actions of American Colonel George Rogers Clark, who exacted revenge on a group of Native Americans.

The rest were surrounded and taken bound to the village where, being set in the street opposite the fort gate, they were put to death, notwithstanding a truce at that moment existed. . . . One of them was tomahawked immediately. The rest, sitting on the ground in a ring, bound, seeing by the fate of their comrade what they had to expect, the next on his left sung his death song and was in turn tomahawked. The rest underwent the same. . . . One only was saved by the intercession of a rebel officer who pleaded for him, telling colonel Clark that the savage's father had formerly saved his life.

The chief of this party, after having the hatchet stuck in his head, took it out himself and delivered it to the inhuman monster who struck him first, who repeated his stroke a second and a third time, after which the miserable spectacle was dragged by the rope around his neck to the river, thrown in, and suffered to spend still a few moments of life in fruitless strugglings. . . .

Colonel Clark, yet reeking with the blood of these unhappy victims, came to the esplanade before the fort gate, where I had agreed to meet him and treat of the surrender of the garrison. He spoke with rapture of his late achievement, while he washed the blood from his hand stained in this inhuman sacrifice.

From Milton Meltzer, ed., *The American Revolutionaries: A History in Their Own Words, 1750–1800.* New York: Thomas Y. Crowell, 1987.

Document 18: Sarah Osborn

Sarah Osborn worked alongside her blacksmith husband, a New York enlistee, through the Revolutionary War. In 1837 she applied for a war widow's pension and her complete involvement came out in her testimony, excerpted here. (Osborn is referred to as a "Deponent".)

Deponent's attention was arrested by the appearance of a large plain between them and Yorktown and an entrenchment thrown up. . . . Deponent took her stand just back of the American tents, say about a mile from the town, and busied herself washing, mending, and cooking for the soldiers, in which she was assisted by the other females; some men washed their own clothing. She heard the roar of the artillery for a number of days, and the last night the Americans threw up entrenchments; it was a misty, foggy night, rather wet but not rainy. Every soldier threw up for himself, as she understood, and she afterward saw and went into the entrenchments. Deponent's said husband was there throwing up entrenchments, and Deponent cooked and carried in beef, and bread, and coffee (in a gallon pot) to the soldiers in the entrenchment.

On one occasion when Deponent was thus employed carrying provisions, she met General Washington who asked her if she "was not afraid of the cannonballs?"

She replied, "No, the bullets would not cheat the gallows," that "It would not do for the men to fight and starve, too."

They dug entrenchments nearer and nearer to Yorktown every night or two till the last. While digging that, the enemy fired very heavy till about nine o'clock next morning, then stopped, and the drums from the enemy beat excessively. . . .

The drums continued beating, and all at once the officers hurrahed and swung their hats, and the Deponent asked them, "What is the matter now?"

One of them replied, "Are not you soldier enough to know what it means?"

Deponent replied, "No."

They then replied, "The British have surrendered."

Deponent, having provisions ready, carried the same down the entrenchments that morning, and four of the soldiers whom she was in the habit of cooking for ate their breakfasts.

Deponent stood on one side of the road and the American officers upon the other side when the British officers came out of the town and rode up to the American officers and delivered up their swords, which the Deponent thinks were returned again, and the British officers rode right on before the army, who marched out beating and playing a melancholy tune, their drums covered with black handkerchiefs and their fifes with black ribbons tied around them, into an old field and there grounded their arms and then returned into town again to await their destiny. Deponent recollects seeing a great many American officers, some on horseback and some on foot, but cannot call them all by name. Washington, Lafayette, and Clinton were among the number. The British general at the head of the army was a large, portly man, full face, and the tears rolled down his cheeks as he passed along.

From Milton Meltzer, ed., *The American Revolutionaries: A History in Their Own Words, 1750–1800*. New York: Thomas Y. Crowell, 1987.

Document 19: Two Views

The rancor between Loyalist (Tory) and Patriot (Whig) supporters was reflected in conduct on both sides characterized by cruelty matched only in the midst of warfare. Here are two views of the conflict. The first is excerpted from an account by Patriot Moses Hall. The second from soldier William Pierce.

The evening after our battle with the Tories, we having a considerable number of prisoners, I recollect a scene which made a lasting impression upon my mind. I was invited by some of my comrades to go and see some of the prisoners. We went to where six were standing together. Some discussion taking place, I heard some of our men cry out, "Remember Buford" [site of a Tory atrocity], and the prisoners were immediately hewed to pieces with broadswords. At first I bore the scene without any emotion, but upon a moment's reflection, I felt such horror as I never did before nor have since, and, returning to my quarters and throwing myself upon my blanket, I contemplated the cruelties of war until overcome and unmanned by a distressing gloom from which I was not relieved by until commencing our march next morning before day by moonlight. I came to Tarleton's camp, which he had just abandoned, leaving lively rail fires. Being on the left of the road as we marched along, I discovered lying upon the ground something with the appearance of a man. Upon approaching him, he proved to be a youth about sixteen who, having come out to view the British through curiosity, for fear he might give information to our troops, they had run him through with a bayonet and left him for dead. Though able to speak, he was mortally wounded. The sight of this unoffending boy, butchered rather than be encumbered in the [illegible] on the march, I assume, relieved me of my distressful feelings for the slaughter of the Tories, and I desired nothing so much as the opportunity of participating in their destruction.

*   *   *   *   *

Such scenes of desolation, bloodshed and deliberate murder, I never was a witness to before! Wherever you turn the weeping widow and fatherless child pour out their melancholy tales to wound the feelings of humanity. The two opposite principles of Whiggism and Toryism have set the people of this country to cutting each other's throats, and scarce a day passes but some poor deluded Tory is put to death at his door. For the want of civil government, the bands of society are totally disunited, and the people, by copying the manners of the British, have become perfectly savage.

From Milton Meltzer, ed., *The American Revolutionaries: A History in Their Own Words, 1750–1800*. New York: Thomas Y. Crowell, 1987.

Document 20: A Warning

Some Loyalists actively retaliated against revolutionaries' violence. To avenge a Loyalist's murder, this note was pinned to the body of John Clark, a known Patriot, in Fishkill, New York.

MARCH 26, 1779

A WARNING TO THE REBELS—You are hereby warned at your peril to desist from hanging any more friends to government as you did Claudius Smith. You are warned likewise to use James Smith, James Flewwelling, and William Cole well, and ease them of their Irons, for we are determined to hank six for one, for the blood of the innocent cries aloud for vengeance. Your noted friend Capt. Williams and his crew of robbers and murderers we have got in our power, and the blood of Claudius Smith shall be repaid. There are particular companies of us who belong to Col. Butler's army, Indians as well as white men, and particularly numbers from New York that are resolved to be avenged on you for your cruelty and murder. We are to remind you, that you are the beginners and aggressors, for by your cruel oppressions and bloody actions, you drive us to it. This is the first, and we are determined to pursue it on your heads and leaders to the last—till the whole of you are murdered.

Stanley I. Kutler, *Looking for America: The People's History*. Vol. 1. New York: W.W. Norton, 1979.

Document 21: Benjamin Franklin's Reflections

After the signing of the Treaty of Paris, many Patriots assessed the waste and devastation of the war with shock. Benjamin Franklin calculated the cost of the previous ten years in lives and missed opportunities.

I join with you most cordially in rejoicing at the return of peace. I hope it will be lasting, and that mankind will, at length, as they call themselves reasonable creatures, have reason and sense enough to settle their differences without cutting throats: For in my opinion, there never was a good war or a bad peace. What vast additions to the conveniences and comforts of living might mankind have acquired, if the money spent in wars had been employed in works of public utility! What an extension of agriculture, even to the tops of our mountains; what rivers rendered navigable or joined by canals; what bridges, aqueducts, new roads, and other public works, edifices, and improvements rendering England a complete paradise, might have been obtained by spending those millions on doing good, which in the last war have been spent in doing mischief; in bringing misery into thousands of families, and destroying the lives of so many thousands of working people, who might have performed the useful labor!

From Milton Meltzer, ed., *The American Revolutionaries: A History in Their Own Words, 1750–1800.* New York: Thomas Y. Crowell, 1987.

Document 22: The Articles of Confederation

The Articles of Confederation, ratified in 1781, established the first U.S. government, but its weaknesses and shortcomings caused leaders to call for its modification almost immediately.

I. The stile of this Confederacy shall be 'The United States of America'.

II. Each state retains its sovereignty, freedom, and independence, and every power, jurisdiction, and right, which is not by this Confederation expressly delegated to the United States, in Congress assembled.

III. The said states hereby severally enter into a firm league of friendship with each other, for their common defence, the security of their liberties, and their mutual and general welfare, binding themselves to assist each other, against all force offered to, or attacks made upon them, or any of them, on account of religion, sovereignty, trade, or any other pretence whatever. . . .

Freedom of speech and debate in Congress shall not be impeached or questioned in any court or place out of Congress, and the members of Congress shall be protected in their persons from arrests and imprisonments, during the time of their going to and from, and attendance on Congress, except for treason, felony, or breach of the peace. . . .

XIII. Every state shall abide by the determinations of the United States in Congress assembled, on all questions which by this confederation are submitted to them. And the Articles of this Confederation shall be inviolably observed by every state, and the

union shall be perpetual; nor shall any alteration at any time here-
after be made in any of them; unless such alteration be agreed to
in a Congress of the United States, and be afterwards confirmed
by the legislatures of every state.

And Whereas it hath pleased the Great Governor of the World
to incline the hearts of the legislatures we respectively represent in
Congress, to approve of, and to authorize us to ratify the said articles of confederation and perpetual union. Know Ye that we the
undersigned delegates, by virtue of the power and authority to us
given for that purpose, do by these presents, in the name and in
behalf of our respective constituents, fully and entirely ratify and
confirm each and every of the said articles of confederation and
perpetual union, and all and singular the matters and things
therein contained: And we do further solemnly plight and engage
the faith of our respective constituents, that they shall abide by the
determinations of the United States in Congress assembled, on all
questions, which by the said confederation are submitted to them.
And that the articles thereof shall be inviolably observed by the
states we respectively represent, and that the union shall be perpetual. In Witness whereof we have hereunto set our hands in
Congress. Done at Philadelphia in the state of Pennsylvania the
ninth day of July, in the year of our Lord one Thousand seven
Hundred and Seventy-eight, and in the third year of the independence of America.

Samuel Eliot Morison, *Sources and Documents Illustrating the American Revolution, 1764–1788, and the Formation of the Federal Constitution*. London: Oxford University Press, 1929.

Document 23: Constitutional Convention Debates

*During the debates at the Constitutional Convention, every minute de-
tail of the government needed to be discussed. In this selection, what powers should be allowed the executive branch was brought forward and debated. The selection shows the position that Benjamin Franklin held at
the Convention.*

MR. PINCKNEY was for a vigorous Executive but was afraid the Executive powers of the existing Congress might extend to peace and
war.

MR. WILSON moved that the Executive consist of a single person. MR. C. PINCKNEY seconded the motion, so as to read "that a
National Executive to consist of a single person, be instituted."

A considerable pause ensuing and the Chairman asking if he
should put the question, DR. FRANKLIN observed that it was a

point of great importance and wished that the gentlemen would deliver their sentiments on it before the question was put.

MR. RUTLEDGE said he was for vesting the Executive power in a single person, though he was not for giving him the power of war and peace. A single man would feel the greatest responsibility and administer the public affairs best.

Ralph Ketcham, ed., *The AntiFederalist Papers and the Constitutional Convention Debates*. New York: New American Library, A Mentor Book, 1986, p. 42.

Document 24: Madison Questions the Power of the Convention

Even among those convention members who were involved in the writing of the Constitution, views were not always positive. In this letter from James Madison to George Washington, Madison wrote about the concern that the Congress did not have the power to write the new Constitution.

It was first urged that as the new Constitution was more than an Alteration of the Articles of Confederation under which Congress acted, and even subverted these articles altogether, there was a Constitutional impropriety in their taking any positive agency in the work. The answer given was that the Resolution of Congress in Feby. had recommended the Convention as the best mean of obtaining a firm *national Government*; that as the powers of the convention were defined by their Commissions in nearly the same terms with the powers of Congress given by the Confederation on the subject of alterations, Congress were not more restrained from acceding to the new plan, than the Convention were from proposing it. If the plan was within the powers of the Convention it was within those of Congress; if beyond those powers, the same necessity which justified the Convention would justify Congress; and a failure of Congress to Concur in what was done, would imply either that the convention had done wrong in exceeding their powers, or that the Government proposed was in itself liable to insuperable objections; that such an inference would be the more natural, as Congress had never scrupled to recommend measures foreign to their constitutional functions, whenever the public good seemed to require it; and had in several instances, particularly in the establishment of the new Western Governments, exercised assumed powers of a very high & delicate nature, under motives infinitely less urgent than the present state of our affairs.

The Debate on the Constitution: Federalist and Antifederalist Speeches, Articles, and Letters During the Struggle over Ratification. New York: The Library of America, 1990, p. 42.

Document 25: Reactions to the Constitution

Americans' reaction to the United States Constitution was varied. This anonymous author, called "Brutus," expressed his doubts that a nation as vast as the United States could be governed as a republic.

History furnishes no example of a free republic, any thing like the extent of the United States. The Grecian republics were of small extent; so also was that of the Romans. Both of these, it is true, in process of time, extended their conquests over large territories of country; and the consequence was, that their governments were changed from that of free governments to those of the most tyrannical that ever existed in the world.

Not only the opinion of the greatest men, and the experience of mankind, are against the idea of an extensive republic, but a variety of reasons may be drawn from the reason and nature of things, against it. In every government, the will of the sovereign is the law. In despotic governments, the supreme authority being lodged in one, his will is law, and can be as easily expressed to a large extensive territory as to a small one. In a pure democracy the people are the sovereign, and their will is declared by themselves; for this purpose they must all come together to deliberate, and decide. This kind of government cannot be exercised, therefore, over a country of any considerable extent; it must be confined to a single city, or at least limited to such bounds as that the people can conveniently assemble, be able to debate, understand the subject submitted to them, and declare their opinion concerning it.

In a free republic, although all laws are derived from the consent of the people, yet the people do not declare their consent by themselves in person, but by representatives, chosen by them, who are supposed to know the minds of their constituents, and to be possessed of integrity to declare this mind.

In every free government, the people must give their assent to the laws by which they are governed. This is the true criterion between a free government and an arbitrary one. The former are ruled by the will of the whole, expressed in any manner they may agree upon; the latter by the will of one, or a few. If the people are to give their assent to the laws, by persons chosen and appointed by them, the manner of the choice and the number chosen, must be such, as to possess, be disposed, and consequently qualified to declare the sentiments of the people; for if they do not know, or are not disposed to speak the sentiments of the people, the people do not govern, but the sovereignty is in a few. Now, in a large extended country, it is impossible to have a representation, possessing the sentiments, and of integrity, to declare the minds of the people, without having it so numerous and unwieldy, as to be subject in great measure to the inconveniency of a democratic government.

The territory of the United States is of vast extent; it now contains near three millions of souls, and is capable of containing much more than ten times that number. Is it practicable for a country, so large and so numerous as they will soon become, to elect a representation, that will speak their sentiments, without their becoming so numerous as to be incapable of transacting business? It certainly is not.

In a republic, the manners, sentiments, and interests of the people should be similar. If this be not the case, there will be a constant clashing of opinions; and the representatives of one part will be continually striving against those of the other. This will retard the operations of government, and prevent such conclusions as will promote the public good. If we apply this remark to the condition of the United States, we shall be convinced that it forbids that we should be one government. The United States includes a variety of climates. The productions of the different parts of the union are very variant, and their interests, of consequence, diverse. Their manners and habits differ as much as their climates and productions; and their sentiments are by no means coincident. The laws and customs of the several states are, in many respects, very diverse, and in some opposite; each would be in favor of its own interests and customs, and, of consequence, a legislature, formed of representatives from the respective parts, would not only be too numerous to act with any care or decision, but would be composed of such heterogenous and discordant principles, as would constantly be contending with each other.

The laws cannot be executed in a republic, of an extent equal to that of the United States, with promptitude.

The magistrates in every government must be supported in the execution of the laws, either by an armed force, maintained at the public expence for that purpose; or by the people turning out to aid the magistrate upon his command, in case of resistance.

Ralph Ketcham, ed., *The Antifederalist Papers and the Constitutional Convention Debates.* New York: New American Library, A Mentor Book, 1986, p. 277.

Document 26: The Rights of Man

Thomas Paine could be considered the mouthpiece of the American Revolution from his work in Common Sense. *But after the Revolution was over and order needed to be restored, Paine took his revolutionary thoughts to France and added his intellectual ability to the French movement. His* The Rights of Man *spoke to the rights of individuals to overthrow their government.*

If there is any thing in monarchy which we people of America do not understand, I wish Mr. Burke would be so kind as to inform us. I see in America, a government extending over a country ten times as large as England, and conducted with regularity for a fortieth part of the expense which government costs in England. If I ask a man in America, if he wants a king, he retorts, and asks me if I take him for an idiot. How is it that this difference happens? Are we more or less wise than others I see in America, the generality of the people living in a style of plenty unknown in monarchial countries; and I see that the principle of its government, which is that of the *equal Rights of Man*, is making a rapid progress in the world.

If monarchy is a useless thing, why is it kept up any where? and if a necessary thing, how can it be dispensed with? That *civil government* is necessary, all civilized nations will agree; but civil government is republican government. All that part of the government of England which begins with the office of constable, and proceeds through the departments of magistrate, quarter-session, and general assize, including the trial by jury, is republican government. Nothing of monarchy appears in any part of it, except the name which William the Conqueror imposed upon the English, that of obliging them to call him "their Sovereign Lord the King."

Edmund Burke and Thomas Paine, *Two Classics of the French Revolution: Reflections on the Revolution in France and The Rights of Man.* New York: Anchor Books/Doubleday, 1989, p. 365.

Document 27: A French View

Alexis de Tocqueville, a French nobleman, was one of the most well known writers in both North America and France. Between the years 1835 and 1856, he wrote two of the most important works on the outcomes of the American and French Revolutions. The first selection from Democracy in America *compares the executive power as it developed in the United States and France. The second selection, from* The Old Regime and the French Revolution, *discusses the role of religion in the United States.*

I

The executive power has so important an influence on the des-

tinies of nations that I wish to dwell for an instant on this portion
of my subject in order more clearly to explain the part it sustains
in America. In order to form a clear and precise idea of the position of the President of the United States it may be well to com-
pare it with that of one of the constitutional kings of France. In
this comparison I shall pay but little attention to the external signs
of power, which are more apt to deceive the eye of the observer
than to guide his researches. When a monarchy is being gradually
transformed into a republic, the executive power retains the titles,
the honors, the etiquette, and even the funds of royalty long after
its real authority has disappeared. The English, after having cut off
the head of one king, and expelled another from his throne, were
still wont to address the successors of those princes only upon their
knees. On the other hand, when a republic falls under the sway of
a single man, the demeanor of the sovereign remains as simple and
unpretending as if his authority was not yet paramount. When the
emperors exercised an unlimited control over the fortunes and the
lives of their fellow citizens, it was customary to call them Caesar
in conversation; and they were in the habit of supping without for-
mality at their friends' houses. It is therefore necessary to look
below the surface.

The sovereignty of the United States is shared between the
Union and the states, while in France it is undivided and compact;
hence arises the first and most notable difference that exists between the President of the United States and the King of France.
In the United States the executive power is as limited and exceptional as the sovereignty in whose name it acts; in France it is as
universal as the authority of the state. The Americans have a Federal and the French a national government.

II

I have sometimes asked Americans whom I chanced to meet in their
own country or in Europe whether in their opinion religion contributed to the stability of the State and the maintenance of law and
order. They always answered, without a moment's hesitation, that a
civilized community, especially one that enjoys the benefits of freedom, cannot exist without religion. In fact, an American sees in religion the surest guarantee of the stability of the State and the safety
of individuals. This much is evident even to those least versed in
political science. Yet there is no country in the world in which the
boldest political theories of the eighteenth-century philosophers
are put so effectively into practice as in America. Only their anti-

religious doctrines have never made any headway in that country, and this despite the unlimited freedom of the press.

I. Alexis de Tocqueville, *Democracy in America*. New York: Vintage Classics/Vintage Books, A Division of Random House, Inc., 1990, p. 123. II. Alexis de Tocqueville, *The Old Regime and the French Revolution*. Garden City, NY: Doubleday & Company, Inc., translated by Stuart Gilbert, p. 153.

Chronology

1763
End of the French and Indian War (Seven Years' War)

1764
Sugar Act and Currency Act passed by British Parliament prompting the first significant protests by American colonists.

1765
Quartering Act and Stamp Act passed by British Parliament; the Sons of Liberty are organized in Boston to protest the British legislation; the Stamp Act Congress meets to coordinate colonial response.

1766
Stamp Act is repealed by Parliament, which then passes, on the same day, the Declaratory Act; New York resistance to the Quartering Act becomes violent and Parliament suspends the New York Assembly.

1767
Townshend Acts are passed by Parliament; colonies respond to increased taxation by supporting a nonimportation policy; John Dickinson writes "Letters from a Farmer in Pennsylvania to the Inhabitants of the British Colonies," which declares the taxation unconstitutional under British law.

1768
Samuel Adams, one of the leaders of the Sons of Liberty in Boston, attacks Parliament's taxation policy in a circular to all colonial leaders.

1769
Virginia House of Burgesses passes resolutions condemning oppressive British actions.

1770
In response to colonial protests, Parliament rescinds the majority of the taxes in the Townshend Acts; colonies in turn relax the policy of nonimportation; rioting between Sons of Liberty in New York and British soldiers over the Quartering Act turns violent, and several colonists are seriously wounded.

March 5 Three colonists are killed in the Boston Massacre; the British soldiers responsible are tried for murder but convicted of lesser charges.

1772
Colonists in Rhode Island attack the British customs schooner *Gaspée*; British officials want to try the culprits in England, further angering the colonists; Samuel Adams organizes the Committee of Correspondence to communicate Boston's position on parliamentary issues to the other colonies, inspiring similar colonial committees.

1773
Tea Act is passed by Parliament; many outraged colonists plan to boycott British tea altogether.

December 16 A Boston mob throws all of the tea on British ships into the harbor; the Boston Tea Party focuses the complete attention of the British Empire on the populace of Boston.

1774
In response to the Boston Tea Party, Parliament passes the Coercive Acts (called the Intolerable Acts in the colonies), and expands the provisions of the Quartering Act; colonial leaders call for a congress to discuss a common response and organize resistance to the recent legislation.

September 5 The First Continental Congress meets in Philadelphia; twelve of thirteen colonies are represented (Georgia is not), and the congress urges all Americans to boycott British goods; British troops begin fortifications in Boston and New England colonial leaders brace for armed conflict; the minutemen are organized.

1775
Parliament passes the New England Restraining Act; General Gage is authorized to use whatever means necessary to gain control of the rebellious colonies; colonial militia resists the British army at the Battles of Lexington and Concord; colonial forces capture the forts and arsenals at Ticonderoga; Green Mountain Boys defeat the British at the Battle of Crown Point; Second Continental Congress meets in Philadelphia and names George Washington, a former British army officer and Virginia planter, as commander-in-chief of the Continental Army.

June 12 Gage orders British ships and troops to attack American fortifications outside Boston; American troops repel several charges but are overrun; Congress issues the Olive Branch Petition to ask King George III to intervene personally in the conflict; there is no immediate response; Congress appoints commissioners to negotiate peace treaties with the Native American tribes to ensure their loyalty, creates a navy and sanctions privateering against the British navy, and actively begins to look to Europe for assistance.

December Canadian expedition fails and Continental Army morale falls.

1776
Thomas Paine publishes *Common Sense*; Congress authorizes the colonies to write their own state constitutions.

July 4 Formal signing of the Declaration of Independence.

August Thirty thousand British troops arrive in New York, engaged by Washington's forces in the Battles of Long Island, Harlem Heights, and White Plains, all defeats for the Americans; Washington defeats British and Hessian troops at Trenton and Princeton.

1777
Congress presents the new flag of the United States; thirteen stripes of red and white and thirteen white stars on a blue field; British attack Philadelphia as Congress flees the city; American forces defeat the British at Saratoga; some American military leaders, led by Thomas Conway, present a letter in Congress critical of Washington's leadership in the war; Conway later resigns and apologizes for the letter; Articles of Confederation are drafted; Washington's army winters at Valley Forge.

1778
Treaties of Alliance and Commerce are signed with France; British officials attempt to make peace but are rejected by American leadership when the issue of independence is dropped; British begin campaign in the South at Savannah.

1779
Spain joins the war on the side of the Americans and the French in hopes of gaining Gibraltar; John Paul Jones gains many victories on the English coast.

1780
British forces take Charleston, South Carolina; American general Benedict Arnold plots to turn West Point over to the British; after his plans fail, he flees to the British and fights against the Americans; American forces are defeated at the Battle of King's Mountain; De Rochambeau arrives from France with 5,500 men to help the American cause.

1781
Articles of Confederation are ratified; a powerful French fleet arrives in America to contend with the British navy; General Greene retakes most of South Carolina and Georgia from the British.

October General Cornwallis is attacked at Yorktown and surrenders the entirety of his forces, more than eight thousand men; British hopes of winning the war are ended.

1782
Peace negotiations begin in Paris among the British, French, and U.S. commissioners.

1783
Congress ratifies the Treaty of Paris; Loyalists and British evacuate the colonies; Washington officially resigns his commission and the Continental Army is disbanded.

For Further Research

Willi Paul Adams, *The First American Constitutions: Republican Ideology and the Making of the State Constitutions in the Revolutionary Era*. Trans. Rita Kimber and Robert Kimber. Chapel Hill: University of North Carolina Press, 1980.

Catherine L. Albanese, *Sons of the Fathers: The Civil Religion of the American Revolution*. Philadelphia: Temple University Press, 1976.

Charles M. Andrews, *The Colonial Background of the American Revolution: Four Essays in American Colonial History*. Rev. ed. New Haven, CT: Yale University Press, 1931.

Bernard Bailyn, *The Ideological Origins of the American Revolution*. Cambridge, MA: Belknap Press of Harvard University Press, 1967.

———, *Origins of American Politics*. New York: Vintage Books, 1967.

Bernard Bailyn and John Hench, eds., *The Press and the American Revolution*. Boston: Northeastern University Press, 1980.

John Edwin Bakeless, *Turncoats, Traitors, and Heroes*. New York: Da Capo Press, 1998.

John Berens, *Providence and Patriotism in Early America, 1640–1815*. Charlottesvile: University Press of Virginia, 1978.

Colin Bonwick, *The American Revolution*. Charlottesville: University Press of Virginia, 1991.

———, *English Radicals and the American Revolution*. Chapel Hill: University of North Carolina Press, 1977.

Daniel Boorstin, *The Americans: The Colonial Experience*. New York: Vintage Books, 1958.

Jerald Brauer, ed., *Religion and the American Revolution*. Philadelphia: Fortress Press, 1976.

Richard Brown, *Knowledge Is Power: The Diffusion of Information in Early America, 1700–1865*. New York: Oxford University Press, 1989.

Robert Brown, *Middle Class Democracy and the Revolution in Massachusetts, 1691–1780*. New York: Harper and Row, 1966.

Edward J. Cashin, *The King's Ranger: Thomas Brown and the American Revolution on the Southern Frontier*. New York: Fordham University Press, 1999.

Ian R. Christie, *Wars and Revolutions: Britain, 1760–1815*. Cambridge, MA: Harvard University Press, 1982.

Ian R. Christie and Benjamin W. Labaree, *Empire or Independence, 1760–1776: A British-American Dialogue on the Coming of the American Revolution*. New York: Norton, 1976.

H. Trevor Colbourn, *The Lamp of Experience: Whig History and the Intellectual Origins of the Revolution*. New York: W.W. Norton, 1965.

Edward Countryman, *The American Revolution*. New York: Hill and Wang, 1985.

Thomas J. Curry, *The First Freedoms*. New York: Oxford University Press, 1986.

Philip Davidson, *Propaganda and the American Revolution*. Chapel Hill: University of North Carolina Press, 1941.

Elisha P. Douglass, *Rebels and Democrats: The Struggle for Equal Political Rights and Majority Rule During the American Revolution*. Chapel Hill: University of North Carolina Press, 1955.

Steven M. Dworetz, *The Unvarnished Doctrine: Locke, Liberalism, and the American Revolution*. Durham, NC: Duke University Press, 1990.

Marc Egnal, *A Mighty Empire: The Origins of the American Revolution*. Ithaca, NY: Cornell University Press, 1988.

Jack P. Greene, ed., *The American Revolution: Its Character and Limits*. New York: New York University Press, 1978.

Robert Gross, *The Minutemen and Their World*. New York: Hill and Wang, 1976.

Thomas O'Brien Hanley, *The American Revolution and Religion: Maryland, 1770–1800*. Washington, DC: Catholic University of America Press, Consortium Press, 1971.

H. James Henderson, *Party Politics in the Continental Congress*. New York: McGraw-Hill, 1974.

Don Higginbotham, *The War of American Independence: Military Attitudes, Policies, and Practice, 1763–1789*. New York: Macmillan, 1971.

Peter Charles Hoffer, *Revolution and Regeneration: Life Cycle and the Historical Vision of the Generation of 1776.* Athens: University of Georgia Press, 1983.

Ronald Hoffman and Peter J. Albert, eds., *The Transforming Hand of Revolution: Reconsidering the American Revolution as a Social Movement: Perspectives on the American Revolution.* Charlottesville, VA: United States Capitol Historical Society, University Press of Virginia, 1995.

Richard Hofstadter, *America at 1750: A Social Portrait.* New York: Vintage Books, 1973.

Rhys Isaac, *The Transformation of Virginia, 1740–1790.* New York: W.W. Norton, 1982.

Michael Kammen, *A Season of Youth: The American Revolution and the Historical Imagination.* New York: Knopf, 1978.

Rosemary Keller, *Patriotism and the Female Sex: Abigail Adams and the American Revolution.* Brooklyn, NY: Carlson, 1994.

David C. King, *Benedict Arnold and the American Revolution.* Woodbridge, CT: Blackbirch Press, 1999.

Lester D. Langley, *The Americas in the Age of Revolution, 1750–1850.* New Haven, CT: Yale University Press, 1996.

Michael Lee Lanning, *Defenders of Liberty: African Americans in the Revolutionary War.* Secaucus, NY: Carol, 1999.

Donald S. Lutz, *Popular Consent and Popular Control: Whig Political Theory in the Early State Constitutions.* Baton Rouge: Louisiana State University Press, 1980.

Stanley Mack, *Stan Mack's Real Life in the American Revolution: The Sweep of History Told in Colorful Detail.* New York: Avon Books, 1994.

Pauline Maier, *The Old Revolutionaries: Political Lives in the Age of Samuel Adams.* New York: Knopf, 1980.

Cathy D. Matson and Peter S. Onuf, *A Union of Interests: Political and Economic Thought in Revolutionary America.* Lawrence: University Press of Kansas, 1990.

Forrest McDonald, *E Pluribus Unum: The Formation of the American Republic, 1776–1790.* 2nd ed., Indianapolis: Liberty Press, 1979.

Robert Middlekauff, *The Glorious Cause: The American Revolution,*

1763–1789. Vol. 2 of the *Oxford History of the United States.* New York: Oxford University Press, 1982.

Edmund S. Morgan, *The Birth of the Republic, 1763–1789.* Chicago: University of Chicago Press, 1977.

Gary B. Nash, *The Urban Crucible: Social Change, Political Consciousness, and the Origins of the American Revolution.* Cambridge, MA: Harvard University Press, 1979.

Gilman Marston Ostrander, *Republic of Letters: The American Intellectual Community.* Madison, WI: Madison House, 1998.

John W. Pulis, ed., *Moving On: Black Loyalists in the Afro-Atlantic World.* New York: Garland Press, 1999.

Thomas L. Purvis, *Revolutionary America, 1763–1800.* New York: Facts On File, 1995.

Paul A. Rahe, *Republics Ancient and Modern: Classical Republicanism and the American Revolution.* Chapel Hill: University of North Carolina Press, 1992.

John Phillip Reid, *Constitutional History of the American Revolution: The Authority of Rights.* Madison: University of Wisconsin Press, 1986.

Boyd Stanley Schlenther, *Charles Thomson: A Patriot's Pursuit.* Newark: University of Delaware Press, 1990.

John Shy, *A People Numerous and Armed.* New York: Oxford University Press, 1976.

R.C. Simmons, *The American Colonies: From Settlement to Independence.* New York: D. McKay, 1976.

Daniel Blake Smith, *Inside the Great House: Planter Family Life in 18th Century Chesapeake Society.* Ithaca, NY: Cornell University Press, 1980.

Robert W. Tucker and David G. Hendrickson, *The Fall of the First British Empire: Origin of the War of American Independence.* Baltimore: Johns Hopkins University Press, 1982.

Helena Wall, *Fierce Communion: Family and Community in Early America.* Cambridge, MA: Harvard University Press, 1990.

Michael Warner, *Letters of the Republic.* Cambridge, MA: Harvard University Press, 1990.

Morton White, *The Philosophy of the American Revolution.* New York: Oxford University Press, 1978.

Gordon S. Wood, *The Creation of the American Republic*. Chapel Hill: University of North Carolina Press, 1969.

Gordon S. Wood, *The Radicalism of the American Revolution*. New York: Knopf, 1992.

Alfred F. Young, ed., *The American Revolution: Explorations in the History of American Radicalism*. DeKalb: Northern Illinois University Press, 1976.

Rosemarie Zagarri, *A Woman's Dilemma: Mercy Otis Warren and the American Revolution*. Wheeling, IL: Harlan Davidson, 1995.

Index